Stories from the Days of Christopher Columbus

"The Young Lovers from Teruel," page 126.

Stories from the Days of Christopher Columbus

A Multicultural Collection for Young Readers
Collected and retold by

Richard Alan Young
with Judy Dockrey Young

August House Publishers, Inc.
LITTLE ROCK

Published by August House, Inc.,
P.O. Box 3223, Little Rock, Arkansas, 72203,
501-372-5450.

Printed in the United States of America

10 9 8 7 6 5 4 3 2

LIBRARY OF CONGRESS CATALOGING-IN-PUBLICATION DATA

Stories from the days of Christopher Columbus :
a multicultural collection for young readers / collected and retold by
Richard Alan Young with Judy Dockrey Young. — 1st ed.
p.   cm.
Summary: a collection of traditional tales, fables, and legends from the cultures brought
together or affected by the voyages of Columbus, including those of Spain, Portugal, Italy,
and the mainland and island Indian tribes he encountered.
ISBN 0-87483-199-7 (alk. paper) : $17.95
ISBN 0-87483-198-9 (pbk.: alk. paper) : $8.95
1. Tales. [1. Folklore.]
I. Young, Richard Alan, 1946– . II. Young, Judy Dockrey, 1949– .
III. Title.
PZ8.1.Y857St   1992
398'.2—dc20   92-6953

First Edition, 1992

Executive: Liz Parkhurst
Project editor: Kathleen Harper
Design director: Ted Parkhurst
Cover design: Wendell E. Hall
Typography: Lettergraphics / Little Rock
The authors of this collection wish to thank reading consultant Martha Ledbetter and re-
search librarians Janet Watkins and Lucille Pratt.
This book is printed on archival-quality paper which meets the
guidelines for performance and durability of the Committee on
Production Guidelines for Book Longevity of the
Council on Library Resources.

AUGUST HOUSE, INC.   PUBLISHERS   LITTLE ROCK

To the memory of
Homer Harry Young, Ph.D.
(1906–1967)
School of Education, Rice Institute, Houston, Texas

Contents

Preface

In the year 1492, most of the people of Europe and America relied on spoken language instead of written language. Very few people in those days knew how to read or write. Europe had many written languages, but the average man or woman, boy or girl, could not read the languages because there were not many opportunities for people to learn to read. Only a small number of schools existed, and since the printing press was not yet in common use, hand-copied books were too expensive for most people to afford.

On the American continents, the Aztec and Mayan Indians had written languages that used pictures instead of letters; they even had hand-written books of folded bark-paper. Most of the people could not read the pictograms, however, because only a small number of boys, chosen to be priests when they grew up, were given the chance to learn the picture writing.

Without much reading and writing, most people learned all that they knew by watching and listening. Instead of watching stories on television or at the movies or reading them in books, everyone listened to stories told out loud. This book is a collection of stories that were being told in the year 1492 and have since been written down on paper. Because five centuries have passed since then, these stories may not be written exactly the way they were told aloud, and these stories have all been translated into English instead of Spanish, Taino, Aztec, or any of the other languages they came from. But they have been written to sound, as much as possible, the way they sounded five hundred years ago when they were told around a lantern on one of Columbus's ships, or around a campfire onshore, or in a native hut made of grass, or in a great, painted stone palace in the Aztec city of Mexico, or in a whitewashed house back in Europe.

Each of these stories has a short introduction to help set the scene for the story. After you have read them silently to yourself, you will enjoy reading or telling them aloud to others, just as they were told so long ago in the days of Christopher Columbus.

Setting Sail

Five centuries ago three small ships left the Spanish seaport of Palos de Moguer *(PAH-lohss deh Moh-GAIRR)* and sailed southwest to islands off the coast of Africa called the Canary Islands, known for their beautiful singing birds. In the Canaries, the ships made repairs—they were old ships and not very well maintained—and the sailors took on supplies for a longer voyage to the west. Most of the sailors were Europeans from Spain, Italy, and Portugal, but some of the men were black men from nearby Africa, and at least one was from Asia. They were about to sail into unexplored and uncharted ocean on the longest and most dangerous sea voyage ever up to that time.

Why would they go on such a dangerous journey? Their commander had a dream, a great goal he wanted to accomplish. He wanted to sail due west from Europe and reach China by a short sea route.

The commander of this expedition was Christopher Columbus, to use his name the way we say it in English, but when he was a boy back in Genoa, Italy, he had been called by his Italian name, Cristoforo Colombo *(Krees-TOH-foh-roh Koh-LOHM-boh)*. He had been given the title of Admiral of the Ocean Sea by King Ferdinand and

Queen Isabella of Spain, and his men called him by his Spanish name, Cristóbal *(Krees-TOH-bahl)* Colón *(Koh-LOHN)*. Colón, or Columbus, had promised the king and queen he would find the way across the wide, dangerous ocean to China and India and bring back the luxuries European people wanted to buy.

Cotton from Arabia and silk from China made softer and more comfortable clothes than what most Europeans wore; coffee from Arabia and tea from China and India were better to drink than the often dirty water in the rivers and streams of Europe at that time; spices like cinnamon from the Orient made food taste better. The people of Europe were willing to pay a good price for these luxuries, and Columbus and the king and queen wanted to become rich by bringing goods from the Orient back to the countries of Europe.

When the ships were repaired and the food and water for the long trip stowed onboard, the crews of the three ships set sail as due west as they could, not knowing that China was twice as far from Europe as Columbus had guessed, and that two huge continents—North America and South America—stood in their way. The wind blew the ships off course and the ocean currents carried them further south than they had planned. The instruments they used to navigate were not as accurate as the ones used by sailors today, and this also put them off course.

They sailed for a month without so much as a glimpse of land. The sailors knew they had just enough food to last for the return trip home, and they wanted to turn back. But Columbus promised them that they would soon see land and offered a reward to the first sailor to sight it. When the ships' crews went to sleep on the evening of October

11, 1492, they knew that if land was not seen in another day or two they would have to give up and return to Europe.

At two hours past midnight on the starry morning of Friday, October 12, 1492, the three small ships were sailing close together, very much alone in uncharted waters three thousand miles west of the Canary Islands, the last land they had seen. On deck one sailor steered with the tiller, a long pole which turned the ship's rudder. One of the boys on the crew stayed awake all night, singing a song and a prayer as he turned the hourglass each hour to keep the time. High in the forecastle at the front of the *Pinta* stood a man named Rodrigo de Triana *(Roh-DREE-goh deh Tree-AH-nah)*. Looking ahead to the west, he spotted dark shapes on the horizon.

De Triana knew that the horizon on the open sea is always level, and that these dark shapes against the starry sky could be only one thing. The sailors had recently seen birds flying above and tree branches and other plant material floating in the water, two signs that land might be near. De Triana squinted hard into the night until he was sure of what he saw. Then he sang out the words that everyone had wanted to hear for so long:

"¡Tierra! ¡Tierra!" which means, "Land! Land!"

The shouts alerted the watchman down on the deck, who woke the rest of the crew. The sailors quickly lowered all but one of the sails to make the ship slow down. The three ships, the *Pinta* (the "Painted One"), the *Niña* (the "Little Lady"), and the *Santa María* (the "Holy Mary") were sailing close together, and messages shouted from the *Pinta* alerted the other two ships. Their crews lowered their sails also. The ships began to jog back and forth, like people pacing back and forth, eagerly awaiting the dawn.

As the sun rose on October 12th, the sailors and the officers could see dark-skinned people on the shore of the small island. In the weeks to come, they would learn that the natives called the island Guanahaní *(Gwah-nah-hah-NEE)*, and the chain of islands to which it belonged the Lucayas *(Loo-CAH-yahs)*. But for now they knew only that the natives were dark-skinned like the people in the faraway lands of India and China which Columbus had hoped to reach. Columbus incorrectly called this place the *Indies,* and called the people *Indians.*

Columbus, the captains of the other two ships, and many men equipped with weapons went ashore in an armed launch. Columbus carried the royal flag of Spain and the two captains each carried an expedition flag, which had a green cross in the center and the letters F and Y on opposite sides of the cross, standing for Fernando and Isabel. Above each initial was a crown to show that these were the initials of the king and queen.

On Guanahaní, Columbus and his men found beautiful ponds, and many strange trees, plants, and fruits they had never seen before.

The native "Indians," who called themselves Tainos *(Tah-EE-nohs),* came down to meet the launch. It would be weeks before Columbus's men could learn enough of the native language to talk very much with the Tainos, so much of the first meeting was trading and pointing and showing things to each other.

It was warm on the island, even in October, and the Tainos did not wear much clothing. The Spaniards laughed at the Indians for wearing so little, and the Indians laughed at the Spanish, who had on hot, heavy clothing even though they didn't need it in that climate. The Indians had fish, fishing spears made of dried cane with a wooden point, parrot feathers, and cotton thread to trade, but the Spanish wanted only one thing: the Indians' little nose ornaments, which were made of gold. Trading began almost immediately.

For the gold, the Spanish gave the Indians small bells, bright beads, pieces of colorful glass, and even pieces of broken pottery with designs in the ceramic. By European standards this was very unfair, but the Indians enjoyed the things the Spanish gave them in trade, and believed they could get more gold later by trading with the people of the islands we now call Hispaniola and Cuba. So, at least on that first day, everyone was fairly happy with the meeting.

At the end of that fateful day when the people of Europe came into permanent contact with the people of the Americas (whom we call Indians, but who are also called native Americans), everyone returned to his own sleeping place. The Taino Indians went back to their village of fifteen or so grass houses with high roofs. A small fire was built in the firepit in the center of each hut, and the smoke went out the smokehole at the point of the roof. The Tainos settled down and told stories in their own language. The sailors went back to their ships and as they prepared for sleep they passed the time, as always, by telling stories. Across the ocean, in Columbus's hometown of Genoa, Italy, and back in Spain where his family and the other men's wives or sweethearts awaited them, people told stories that same night. And on the mainland of North America, in the Aztec city of Mexico, the Aztec people, as well as other Indians on the mainland, also ended the day with storytelling.

These many people from different continents and cultures, speaking different languages, all had storytelling in common. Their stories were very different, though, and as they passed that first night of this modern age, these were some of the stories they were probably telling.

On Board the Pinta

Back on the three ships in the bay, the Spanish sailors and sailors from other places as well, including Africa and Asia, were still sharing their stories. The ships rocked gently in the waves and the candle–lanterns swung as the sailors told their tales.

Each of Columbus's ships had a story of its own.

*Two of the ships were known by their nicknames instead of their real names. One was the **Pinta.** This nickname probably came from the fact that a former owner had the last name of Pinto, and she was his ship. But now she belonged to the rich and well-known sailing family of Palos, the Pinzón (Peen-SSOHN) family. Sailors also would have thought of the nickname Pinta as meaning "The Painted Lady," and some of her parts may have been brightly painted. It was from the **Pinta** that land had first been sighted that morning, giving the **Pinta** a special place in history.*

*But we do not know the official name of the **Pinta.** It has been forgotten in the five hundred years since she sailed.*

Don Juan Calderón Kills Seven

*On board the **Pinta**, with the candle-lantern swinging slowly back and forth as the ship rocked gently in the surf, the men and boys told stories about heroes. This is the story of one very unusual hero, who never planned on being a hero at all. This story was told all over Europe, with different names and details, but to the Spanish it was "Don Juan Calderón Kills Seven."*

It was that there was, in the years before the many small kingdoms of the Peninsula were united under King Ferdinand and Queen Isabel, in a village high in the Mountains of Moraine in southwestern Spain, there lived a little leatherworker. His house was made of whitewashed stucco with a roof of red tile. The room in back was his home, with a fireplace and a table and a chair and a bed and a great trunk at the foot of the bed where he kept his clothing; the room in front was his shop, with his workbench and his tool chest and a cabinet full of leather, and walls hung with saddles and bridles and other leather goods for sale.

One fine morning he sat at his workbench, making a leather belt for a rich, fat man who lived in the village. Just as he was preparing to tool the designs that the rich man had asked for into the leather, he sat back for a moment and began to think about what he might have for his lunch. He had only finished breakfast a few minutes before, but it was never too early in the day for him to start thinking about lunch. His name was Juan, this little leatherworker, and his family name was Calderón, which means the same as "cooking pot." It was a good name for a plump little man who thought about food a lot. He sat back with his leather hammer in his hand, and began to daydream about his lunch.

"Let's see," thought Juan, "I could have some ham and some bacon and some sausage and some bread and some olive oil and some…" While he was daydreaming, he grew very still. In fact, he did not move any at all. He sat so still that a little housefly, buzzing about above the workbench, forgot that there was a person down below. The fly began to think that Juan was another piece of furniture. (Flies have a very short memory.) The fly flew down to the workbench and began to walk around until it found a little grain of sugar from the sweetbread Juan had eaten for breakfast. Then it called to its fly friends to come down and join it for a fly feast. Six more houseflies flew down and they all gathered, seven in a circle, around the grain of sugar, discussing fly politics or some such matter. Just at that moment, Juan ended his daydream.

"…and I could have some custard with caramel sauce for dessert."

Then he blinked his eyes and looked down for the first time in several minutes. There sat seven rude flies on

Juan's workbench. How insulting! Using the only thing he had in his hand, his leather hammer, Juan took the flies by surprise and killed all seven with one blow. He brushed his workbench clean, and began to talk to himself as he sometimes did when alone.

"You know," he said to himself very proudly, "I imagine that no one else has ever killed seven houseflies with one blow before. I should do something to reward myself for such a great deed. I could use a new belt myself, and the rich man doesn't need this one I'm making until next week. I think I'll make this belt for myself!"

He began to work with his hammer and tools, writing his name on his belt; *J...u...a...n...,* he wrote, *...C...a...l...d...e...r...ó...n.* Since the leatherworker was a plump little man, he had a lot of belt left to write on, so he wrote the words "Kills Seven," in honor of the fact that he had killed seven flies with one blow. Well, he might have written "kills seven houseflies," but not even Juan was plump enough for that many words! But there was still a little bit of room in front of his name, so he wrote the word *Don* meaning "Very Important Mister," in front of his name.

He held up his new belt and read it: "Very Important Mister Juan Calderón Kills Seven." He was very proud of his brave deed and of his new belt, and he decided to go out and show it off to his friends. He put on his brimless leather hat and swung his leather pouch of leatherworking tools over his shoulder. (When he went walking on the streets of his little town, people were always asking him to stop and fix a boot, or stitch up the loose threads on a bridle, or some other thing. Juan enjoyed the copper coins they paid him, and the chance to sit and visit while he worked.) Then he put on his new belt, cinched it tight, and set out to walk to the plaza to see his friends.

First he saw Don Diego, an old retired soldier of fortune, sitting on a bench by the street. "Don Diego," he called out, "look at my new belt," and he turned to show off the writing on the back. Before he could explain about the houseflies, Don Diego had read "Very Important Mister Juan Calderón Kills Seven..." and said, "Don Juan, I did not know that you had killed seven men in combat! I did not even know that you were a veteran!"

Don Juan tried to explain that it was only seven foolish houseflies that he had killed, but it was already too late. The truth runs along the ground like a lizard, but rumor has wings like a hawk. Don Diego was already calling out the news to his friends across the street.

By the time Don Juan had explained it all to Don Diego, seven other men had heard the rumor, and it was "Don Juan Calderón killed seven men in combat." By the time the rumor reached the edge of the plaza, it had grown to "Don Juan Calderón killed seven men in combat with his bare hands." By the time the rumor got to the front door of the cathedral, it had grown to "Don Juan Calderón killed seven men in combat with his bare hands, after the rest of the army had retreated in fear." By the time the rumor got to the marketplace beyond the plaza, it had grown to "Don Juan Calderón killed seven men in combat with his bare hands, after the rest of the army had retreated in fear, in the great battle for the city of Valencia."

No one stopped to remember that the Battle of Valencia had ended over two hundred years before!

A large crowd had gathered around Don Juan in the plaza, congratulating him as he tried to explain that it had only been seven foolish houseflies that he had killed. Just then, a knight in armor rode into the plaza on a great white horse. He dismounted, climbed the steps of the cathedral, and faced the crowd.

"*Señores* and *señoras*," he shouted, "a great tragedy has befallen Spain! The caliph at Granada has sent a giant to kill the king of Spain! We must have a champion who will fight this giant and save the king!"

All the people of the little town shouted at once, "Don Juan Calderón will do it!" And they all cheered, and ten of them picked up the little leatherworker—he was rather heavy—and carried him on their shoulders and placed him on the knight's great war horse. The knight leaped astride the horse and they rode away to the capital city of Toledo, where the king of Spain lived in a great castle.

Don Juan was led into the large hall where the king sat on his throne and greeted his guests. He bowed very low, and waited for the king to speak first.

"Greetings, *Señor*," said the king. "Could it be that you have come to prove yourself as my champion?"

Don Juan bowed low again before he spoke. He wanted to explain that he was only a simple leatherworker, and he had killed only seven houseflies, and he thought the best way was to show off a sample of his work: his new belt he had made for himself.

"Your Majesty," said Don Juan, "as you can see by this belt..." He turned around to show that he was a leatherworker, but the king read the inscription very quickly. Before Don Juan could finish his sentence, the king said,

"Very Important Mister Juan Calderón Kills Seven? Why, *Señor*, my personal bodyguard killed only five men when I led the soldiers in wars against the Moors. You must be a great warrior. I name you my champion!" With that, he laid his shiny sword on Don Juan's shoulder as a sign of the little leatherworker's new rank.

Only moments later, it seemed, Don Juan was marching out the city gates, with forty soldiers escorting him, headed for the grassy plain to meet the giant. "Well," thought the little leatherworker, "this is not so bad. Counting me there must be forty-two or -three of us! I bet that old giant will be quaking in his boots with fear when he..."

But then the soldiers stopped and faced Don Juan, and raised their swords in a salute. Wishing him good luck, the escort went back through the city gates and slammed them shut.

Don Juan Calderón was all alone on the grassy plain by the River Tajo *(TAH-hoh)*.

"Well," thought Don Juan, "this is not so bad. The giant may not come today. He may not even see little me here in the big, empty grassland."

Just then, over the mountains came the biggest giant Don Juan had ever seen, heard of, or imagined in his nightmares. The giant was as tall as seven men would be if they stood on one another's shoulders. The giant wore big black boots as high as a housetop, big, black, puffy pants as big as the sails of a ship, and a big turban for a hat on his head. He carried a huge curved sword as long as three straight Spanish swords laid end-to-end! And he walked onto the grassy plain, right up to Don Juan, and bent down low to look at him.

"WHO ARE YOU?" asked the giant, in a voice like thunder.

The little leatherworker leaned back away from the giant's ugly head, and said, as bravely as he could, "Well, Your Enormousness, I am Juan Calderón…and the king of Spain"—he tried to gather his courage—"has sent me…has sent me…"

"YES?" roared the giant.

"…has sent me to make you a new belt!" It was all Don Juan could think to say.

The giant stood upright again. "GOOD!" he boomed. "SHOW ME A SAMPLE OF YOUR WORK."

"Well," thought Don Juan to himself, "this is not so bad. I will show him this belt, and he will read what it says, and he will think I am a great warrior. He'll probably be shaking in his big black boots when he reads this!" So he turned and bowed down so the giant could read the writing on the belt. The giant stooped very low (for a giant) and looked very closely at the belt, with eyeballs as big as melons.

"Well, Your Giganticness," said the little leatherworker, "What do you think of the inscription?"

"I'M FROM PERSIA," thundered the giant, "I CAN'T READ SPANISH!"

Oh, the poor little leatherworker! Here was the only person in the whole wide world he would like to have fooled with the belt, and the giant couldn't read what it said! Don Juan began to think very fast.

"HOW MANY COWSKINS WILL WE NEED FOR THE BELT?" boomed the giant, eager to receive his gift from, he presumed, the king of Spain.

Well, now, this was something Don Juan was good at! Making things from leather! He looked up at the giant's waist, and thought about it for a moment. "Seven," he called up to the giant. "We will need seven cowskins."

"I'LL BE RIGHT BACK," said the giant, in a voice like waves crashing on the rocks in a storm. And he turned and stomped away, stepping over the mountains as he went.

When he was gone, Don Juan said to himself, "Well, this is not so bad! Now that he's gone, I can run away and...and"—then he knew he could not run—"and I would be a coward, and the people of my village would be so disappointed in me."

So he sat down and waited. He did not have long to wait. Over the mountains came the giant, with three dead cows under one arm and four dead cows under the other.

The giant threw down the cows, and skinned them with his huge curved sword. He dragged the skins over to the little leatherworker, and boomed, "GET TO WORK!"

Don Juan got to work. He opened his pouch of tools and took out his knives, cut each skin into a rectangle, and laid them end-to-end in the grass. He slit the extra skin into long strips, and used an awl to punch holes along the edges of the leather rectangles. He began to stitch the skins together into a huge belt.

"Well," thought Don Juan to himself, "this is not so bad. When he gets this belt on, I'll bet that old giant will be so grateful that he will want to be my friend." So he looked up at the giant and asked in a loud voice, "Oh, excuse me, Your Hugeness, but what shall we do after I finish your nice new belt?"

The giant folded his arms and looked down at Don Juan. "AFTER YOU FINISH THE BELT, I WILL SQUASH YOU WITH MY THUMB!"

Now, if Don Juan were to name all the things he liked to do, being squashed by the thumb of a giant would have been very near the end of the list. Once again, he began to think very fast. "Well, Your Extremely Bigness, it's an awfully hot afternoon. Couldn't we have something to drink?"

"I'LL BE RIGHT BACK," thundered the giant, and he stomped away over the mountain. Don Juan quickly finished lacing the pieces together, completing the huge belt. He grabbed one end and slowly dragged the belt down to the River Tajo, and pushed the enormous belt into the water. He let it soak for a few minutes, then slowly pulled the long, wet, heavy leather strip back out onto the grass.

Just then, the giant came tramping back over the mountains, carrying three barrels of wine under one arm, and four barrels of wine under the other. He dropped the barrels beside the little leatherworker, and used his giant curved sword to cut the tops off all seven barrels. The giant lifted a barrel, and drank from it as if it were a cup. Don Juan took off his brimless leather hat and dipped it into one of the barrels and used it as a cup. While the two were quenching their thirst in the hot, bright afternoon sun, Don Juan suggested, "Why don't you try on your new belt, Your Great Bigness?"

"GOOD IDEA!" the giant bellowed. He stood up, picked up the huge belt, and wrapped it around his waist.

"Tie it good and tight," Don Juan shouted up to the giant who towered over him. The giant tied the belt very tight.

"IT'S WET!" boomed the giant suspiciously.

"Oh, Your Immenseness," said Don Juan, "it was a little dirty, so I washed it off. Let's finish our drink."

The giant sat back down and continued drinking wine in the hot afternoon sun. Pretty soon he began to yawn and blink. After a while, he forgot all about the little leather-worker, and laid down on the grassy plain to take a nap. Don Juan moved over to sit in the shade of the sleeping giant and finish his hatful of wine. The giant began to snore.

Don Juan wiped sweat off his forehead and put his hat on. He stood up and stepped back to survey his work. It was a beautiful belt, with the spotted cow hair to the outside. But it was an ugly giant snoring in the hot sun of afternoon. Slowly the hot sun dried the fresh, wet leather, and it began to shrink. The belt grew tighter and tighter as the leather shrank—tighter and tighter, until it crushed the giant to death!

Don Juan picked up his pouch of tools and walked calmly back to the city gates.

Don Juan was a hero! The entire city came out to see him made a knight of the realm. The king of Spain gave him forty pieces of gold as warrior's pension, and a beautiful red sash that said "Friend of the King" on it. Caballero *(Cah-bahl-YEH-roh)* Juan (for so knights were called) was given a white horse to ride home on.

In his home village up in the foothills he was greeted by a cheering crowd of his friends. Twenty of them picked him up on their shoulders—he was heavier than ever, carrying his bag of gold—and carried him to the plaza, where they sang and danced and ate fine foods and had the biggest feast day the town had ever seen. As the sun was coming up the next day, everyone said, "Good dawn," and went home.

Caballero Juan Calderón went to his little house that he had left early that morning. He hung his red sash in the cabinet in his shop, and went into his bedroom. He took off the belt that had brought him so much trouble, rolled it up, and put it in the trunk at the foot of his bed, and he never, never wore that belt again!

In the Taino Village

In a small grass hut with a high roof, a family of Tainos sat around the firepit, or swung in their hammocks. They ate pineapple, a white bread made of manioc, fish they had caught on their dried reed spears, and sweet potatoes. Other nights they might eat peanuts, squash, and beans, with shellfish or turtle from the shallow tidal lagoons. Sometimes they ate crab meat and corn.

The older men had painted their faces and bodies with black vegetable paint made from the inaja-palm tree, and red paint made from the annatto tree. The language they used to tell their stories would sound strange to us today, but we would recognize some of the words they spoke because even today we use the Taino words maize, potato, barbecue, maraca and canoe. We can see part of the Taino way of life in these words: they went fishing in canoes, they dried and barbecued the fish they caught on a wooden frame, and after eating potatoes and maize (corn), they might sing and dance to the music of the maraca, a kind of rattle made from a gourd.

The Cave of the Inaja-Palm Paint

As the old men told the stories, they taught the young Taino boys and girls about how they saw the world and how they thought it had come into being. Here is their story, "The Cave of the Inaja-Palm Paint."

In the beginning of time, on the nearby Great Island now called Hispaniola, there is a place called Caonao *(COW-now)*. In that old place there is a mountain called Cauta *(CAUGHT-ah)*. In the mountain are two caves.

One cave is black inside, like the black facepaint we make from the fruit of the inaja-palm tree. This is called the "Cave of the Inaja-Palm Paint." From that cave came all our tribe, all the Taino people.

The other cave is called the "Cave of No Importance." From it came all the other, less fortunate people who live in the world.

In the Cave of the Inaja-Palm Paint, the Taino people lived in utter darkness. They had never seen the sun, and were afraid of its light. No one went outside when the sun was hot and bright. The people in the cave even put a guard named He-Who-Does-Not-Blink at the mouth of the cave, to guard against whatever danger might be outside. But one day he did not do his job.

That day, He-Who-Does-Not-Blink was not at the mouth of the cave. Everyone inside said he must have been carried away by the sun. This made the foolish people even more afraid, and they shut the mouth of the cave, like a door. He-Who-Does-Not-Blink came back late, having traveled with the sun, and was turned to stone for his poor job of guarding the entry.

The reason He-Who-Does-Not-Blink was put on guard was to stay awake and make sure that the people did not go out into the "dangerous" bright light. If people did leave the cave, his job was to see where they went and whether or not they came back. His wandering off to travel with the sun was a big mistake on his part, and he was turned to stone as punishment.

Some of the people wanted to go out in the daylight and fish, but when they saw the sun, they were taken prisoner by the sun, and were turned into cherry-plum trees.

One of the people in the cave was named Old One, and he wanted to go out of the cave to get some soap-plant for his bath. He went out before the sun came up, but he stayed too long, and the sun turned him into the songbird that sings at dawn.

But finally a great hero came out of the cave. His name was Proud One, and the people called him that because they were proud of his courage. He told the people to stop being afraid and to go out into the daylight. All the men were afraid, but the women were brave, and agreed to go with him.

Proud One led the women out of the cave in the springtime. The cowardly men stayed behind in the dark, and demanded that the children stay with them. The children cried at night because their mothers went out into the daylight. The children became frogs that sing at night, and are no longer lonely.

And the women that came out of the Cave of the Inaja-Palm Paint became the grandmothers of all of us, and we live now in the daylight and are happy.

On Board the Niña

*Another of Columbus's ships was the **Niña,** and sailors saying this nickname would have thought of "The Little Lady." The nickname probably comes from the fact that the ship was owned by a family with the last name Niño. The true name of the **Niña** was Santa Clara. She was the smallest of the three ships in the fleet, only seventy feet long. The **Niña** was so small that she could float in a modern swimming pool, yet she and her sister ships traveled thousands of miles across open sea, through storms and other dangers, to come to this New World.*

The Cat Who Became a Monk

*On the deck of the **Niña**, some of the sailors gathered to share stories. Perhaps they told this and the following stories, each man or boy taking his turn.*

This is the story of the cat who turned himself into a monk. In one of the monasteries, in the dining hall, there lived a cat who had killed and eaten all the mice except one large mouse which had always escaped him.

One day, the cat thought of a way to catch the mouse. He went to the room where one of the monks lived and got a pair of scissors. He cut a bald patch on the top of his head, which was how the monks wore their hair.

Next, he went to the room where one of the monks was doing the laundry. Without asking, he borrowed one of the robes and put it on.

Then the cat pretended to be a monk. He walked along on his hind legs like a monk and went to prayers with the other monks. At dinnertime, the cat walked in and sat on a bench at the table, just like the other monks.

When the big mouse saw this, he thought, "The cat has become a monk! He will only eat the food prepared for him in the kitchen, like the other monks do. He won't eat me now."

Out came the mouse from his mouse house. He danced along the floor under the monks' table, eating the scraps they dropped by accident. Finally the mouse came right under the feet of the cat.

The cat jumped down and caught the mouse.

"Wait!" said the mouse. "You can't eat me! You're a monk!"

"Clothing doesn't change me," said the cat. "I'm a monk when I want to be and a cat when I don't."

With that, he ate the mouse.

And let that be a lesson to us all!

The men on the ship all laughed at the story about the cat. They knew this kind of story well. Some of the others took turns telling more of the same kind of fables—stories about talking animals that show us the truth about how human beings behave.

The Pig and the Mule

*Soon other men and boys told their favorite fables from this collection of tales known as **The Book of Cats**. Here is another such story.*

Two animals lived on the farmstead of a good man of Spain. The mule worked hard in the fields, side by side with the man, and each evening he was given oats to eat. The pig did no work at all, but just slept and grunted and pushed his nose in the ground sniffing for things to eat. Yet every evening the pig was given all the stale bread and table scraps from the household.

"This pig has an easy life," the mule thought to himself. "He does no work and yet he eats as well as a person. I think I will pretend to be ill, and get myself some special food, too."

The mule lay down as if he were ill. The farmer found him and said, "The mule has fallen ill. We must feed him to make him well."

And feed him they did, with fresh bread and water, ground meal from the kitchen, and green vegetable tops from the garden. At first the mule ate only a little, as if he were really ill. Then, as days went by, he ate more and more and began to grow fat.

Soon winter was coming, and the farmer sent for the butcher to come from the village. The mule watched in horror as the butcher, with an axe and a knife, killed the fattened pig and cut him up for meat.

The mule feared that the farmer would have him butchered next! And he thought to himself, "I would rather work hard in the fields for the rest of my life than be fattened up this fine summer only to be hung up as meat in the pantry in autumn."

With that the mule, pretending to be well from his "illness," ran out of the stable and into the yard where the farmer stood. The mule began to dance about, and sang, "Hee haw! Hee haw!"

The farmer was delighted to see his old mule well again, and the two went right to work. The mule worked hard all his life and never complained again.

And let that be a lesson to us all!

The sailors all laughed again at the story of the mule, even though many of them already knew these stories by heart. Their pleasure was in hearing them again, told by friends, who each added something of his own to them.

The House Mouse
and the Field Mouse

*An old man with only one good eye spoke up and told
another fable from **The Book of Cats.***

There were two mice who were cousins, but one lived
in the farmhouse and the other lived in the
countryside.

It happened that they met in the yard one day, and the
house mouse said, "Greetings, Cousin. Tell me what it is
you eat in the fields every day."

"Wild beans," answered the field mouse, "and wheat
and dried barley grains."

"Well," said the house mouse, "those are rather slim
rations. I am much surprised that you don't waste away
from hunger."

"Tell me, Cousin," said the field mouse, "what is it
you dine on?"

"Well," said the house mouse, "I eat bread and cheese
and fine meat and things that fall from the people's table.

You should join me for supper some evening and we'll dine on the the best!"

This pleased the field mouse very much and he agreed to come to the house that very evening. As the sun went down, the field mouse and the house mouse came out of their mouse hole and into the kitchen where the family sat at the table. They scampered about and ate things that fell to the floor.

Just about that time, along came the fat old cat that lived in the house, and she pounced on the field mouse and almost ate him! He wiggled away and ran for the mouse hole, with his house cousin close behind him.

"What was that?" asked the field mouse.

"Just the cat," said the house mouse. "You get used to her. You should dine with me more often. It would be great fun."

"But doesn't the cat ever catch mice?" gasped the field mouse.

"Oh," said the house mouse, "she ate my father and she ate my mother and has almost eaten me a few times."

"No, thank you," said the field mouse. "I would not wish to gain the whole Mouse World if the danger were that great. I'll stay in the field and eat my grains and beans, and leave you to your fine food and your dinner guest."

As the field mouse went out of the house he said to himself, "I'd rather gnaw on a bean than have fear gnawing on me!"

And let that be a lesson to us all!

The laughter again sounded out over the quiet bay from the little ships.

Lady Owl's Child

"Here's one more of those fables!" said a young man in a brown hat, and he told this story from **The Book of Cats.**

It happened that all the animals called a council among themselves and asked that every kind of animal send a representative to the Court of the Animals. Now, it was a great honor to be selected to go to the Court of the Animals, and the owl was very proud when the nightbirds selected his son to go as their representative.

The owl's son set out—by night, of course—and flew toward the great clearing in the forest where the court was to be held. Only after the son was gone did his mother discover that he had left without putting on his fine new shoes that he had wanted to wear at court.

Lady Owl tried to think of which animal was the fastest so she could send the shoes by way of that animal to get to court as soon as her son arrived. Then he could put on his new shoes.

Lady Owl decided that the rabbit was fastest. She called at the home-in-the-ground of Lady Rabbit and asked her if she were going to court.

"Yes, I am," she replied.

"My son forgot his shoes," said Lady Owl. "Would you take them to him?"

"Of course," replied Lady Rabbit. "How will I know which one is your son?"

Lady Owl answered, "Oh, my son will be the most handsome bird there."

"Then," said Lady Rabbit, "your son must be the dove."

"Oh, no," said Lady Owl.

"Then he must be the peacock!" exclaimed Lady Rabbit.

"Oh, no," said Lady Owl. "He is neither of those birds. Why, the dove is all dark meat, and the peacock has such ugly feet!"

"I'm sorry," said Lady Rabbit. "You'll have to describe your son to me so I'll know which one he is."

"Well," said Lady Owl, "my son has a head just like mine and feathers just like these and feet just like these." She tilted her head, and showed her own wings and feet to Lady Rabbit. "And he'll be the handsomest bird there, and that's who you give the new shoes to."

Lady Rabbit smiled and took the shoes and hopped all the way to the Court of the Animals. She gave the shoes to the owl who was very grateful. Later, Lady Rabbit was talking to King Lion and she told him how Lady Owl had described her son.

"Yes," said old King Lion thoughtfully, "if you're in love with a frog, you think that frog is the moon. If you're in love with a toad, she looks like a queen to you."

And let that be a lesson to us all.

The sailors nodded and smiled at each other. One of them, an older sailor, said to the man who had told the story, "I suspect you've been in love with a toad or two yourself!"

Everyone laughed good–naturedly, even the man who had told the story.

The Example of the Lion and the Rabbit

*"But speaking of King Lion," began the older sailor, clearing his throat, "and the rabbit..." And he told this story, which was one of many in **The Book of Kalil and Dimna.***

Once there was a vicious lion in a faraway land. In this land there was plenty of water and grassland, and many beasts lived there. But these beasts were vicious to one another because of their fear of the lion, who ate one of the beasts each day.

One day the beasts all came together in a council and discussed the lion problem. They talked most of the night, while the lion slept, and by the next morning they had reached an agreement. They sent representatives of each animal to meet with the lion before he became hungry for his midday meal.

"Great Lion," said the beasts, "every time you take one of us it is a great insult and a great affront to us, and we live in fear of you. We have held a council, and we have an offer to make to you.

"If you will leave us alone to eat and drink and go about the grassland in peace each day, then we promise to select one from among us each day, and send him to you at midday as tribute."

This pleased the lion, for it meant he would not have to hunt for his midday meals anymore. He agreed.

This went well for a while, with each kind of animal selecting one of its members to go to the lion as a tribute to be eaten by him, and to keep peace in the land.

One day the rabbits were to send a rabbit as tribute. They drew lots among them, and it fell to a smart, young rabbit to go and be eaten by the lion. The young rabbit was not very happy with the arrangement; he did not especially wish to become a lion's lunch.

"If I may speak a moment before I go," said the rabbit, "I will tell you of a plan that will do you no harm, and in fact will end up doing you good. My plan will allow you all to escape from the tyranny of the lion and it will allow me to escape becoming his lunch."

"What must we do?" the rabbits and all the other animals asked.

"Whoever takes me to the lion," said the rabbit, "must take me very slowly. Let them take so long that by the time we arrive, it will be past the lion's lunchtime. I will do the rest."

"That pleases us," said the animals, and they agreed.

As the sun reached the high point in the sky, the lion grew hungry and angry as his tribute was not on time. He stood up and looked to his right and to his left: no tribute in sight. Soon he began to pace angrily back and forth.

At last, here came the rabbit, hopping very slowly along, and without a procession of animals to escort him to the lion.

"Where is the tribute procession of animals?" demanded the lion. "And why are you so late in arriving? Why have the beasts broken their agreement with me?"

"I am the tribute of the beasts," said the young rabbit, "and I bring you a rabbit for your midday meal—myself. I am sorry to be so late, but another lion saw the tribute procession and told the animals, 'You should give that rabbit to me instead of to the lion you're going to see.'"

"Another lion?" asked the lion suspiciously.

"But I said to him," the rabbit went on, "'No, this rabbit is for the king of the beasts, the lion who is our master, and this rabbit is for his midday meal. You had better not take this rabbit and eat him yourself or the lion, our master, will be very angry.'"

"What other lion?" growled the lion, getting angry.

"But that other lion wouldn't let it go at that," the rabbit continued. "He said, 'Tell that lion, the king of beasts, that I want to fight him.' And with that, he took another of the rabbits from the tribute procession. I came here after all the other beasts had run away. I wanted to come and complain to you about it."

"Go with me," snarled the lion, "and show me where this other lion is."

"Put me under your arm," said the rabbit. "I'll show you where to go."

The lion took the rabbit under one great arm and off they went to a deep, clear pool of water that the rabbit directed the lion to.

"He's in that pool," said the rabbit. "You'd better be careful."

The lion crept to the edge of the deep pool and looked in, and saw his reflection in the water. There was a lion, with an angry look on his face, and a rabbit under his arm!

The king of beasts put the rabbit down and dove into the pool to kill the other lion, not doubting for a moment that there was another lion at the bottom of the pool. Diving deeper and deeper in search of the lion, the king of the beasts was drowned.

And the young rabbit went back to the council of the beasts and told them that the lion was dead, and they had secured their freedom.

On the
Aztec Mainland

Hundreds of miles west of where Columbus's ships lay offshore on the night of October 12, 1492, a great Indian civilization inhabited a wide valley now called the Valley of Mexico. In this valley (where Mexico City sits today) there were lakes in the days of Columbus. On islands in these lakes and on the shores around the lakes were great cities with stone temples and wide streets, plazas and marketplaces, and houses of whitewashed mud brick with roofs of grass thatch. In these cities lived thousands of Aztec Indian people, whom Columbus never saw.

In the Aztec Palace: The Smoking Mountain

On the main island in the middle of the largest lake stood the capital of the Aztec Empire, Tenochtitlán (Teh-nohch-tee-TLAHN), which means "Place of the Aztecs" or "Place of Cactus-on-Stone" in the Aztec language.

In 1520, thirty-eight years after the events in this book, the Spaniards would come and conquer the city of Tenochtitlán and rename it Mexico City. At that time the Aztec chief (also called the king or the emperor) would be Motecuhzoma (Moh-teh-cuh-ZOH-mah) the Second; his people would fight against the Spanish general Cortez. But that would come later.

In one of the palaces of the royal family and the royal priests, young girls dressed in plain cotton dresses sat on reed mats and listened to a storyteller. Their favorite story was being told, a story that has many different versions because so many people have told it so many times.

Long ago, on the banks of the Great Lake in the center of the Valley of Mexico, there were four great kingdoms. To the north was the Black Kingdom, where the temples were painted black, and the warriors painted the top half of their faces black. To the south was the Blue Kingdom, where the palace of the king was painted blue, and everyone showed hospitality to visitors from other lands. To the west was the White Kingdom, where white snow covered the tops of some of the mountains, and white clouds hung in the western sky. To the east was the Red Kingdom, so named for the red sky of dawn in the east and the red flowers that bloomed there.

The most beautiful girl in the Red Kingdom was the daughter of its king, a princess named Yoloxóchitl *(Yoh-loh-SHOH-cheetl)*, which means "Red Flower." Her father had forbidden her to marry until he found a young man that he thought was suitable for her. As you might have guessed, many young men had come to ask his permission to marry Red Flower, but the king had turned them all away. So Red Flower was alone and lonely.

One day Red Flower went for a walk away from the palace to the banks of the Great Lake that lay in the center of the valley. The valley was surrounded by mountains except to the east, where the morning sun poured in, red and beautiful. The rain and melting snow came down from the ring of mountains and formed a shallow lake. Red Flower's people and the people of the other kingdoms often went out onto the lake in reed fishing boats to catch fish. One of these boats sat on the shore where Red Flower was walking. Knowing that all her people loved her and would deny her nothing, she borrowed the reed boat without asking, and paddled out onto the cool lake.

It was evening, and the sun was in the west. The white clouds and the white, snow-covered mountains shone brightly. As Red Flower came near the painted pole that was the boundary marker in the center of the lake, she heard someone singing on the western shore. It was the voice of a young man. Forgetting any danger, and against custom, Red Flower paddled past the painted boundary pole and headed toward the western coast.

As she glided in to the shoreline, a young man stood up from the rock he had been sitting on and came down to her. He was the most handsome man Red Flower had ever seen, and wore a beautiful cape made of white bird feathers. He greeted her very politely as she stepped out of the boat and onto the beach.

"I am Tépetl *(TEH-pehtl),*" he said, "'Strong-like-the-Mountain.' I am the prince of the White Kingdom in the west."

Red Flower introduced herself, and told him how her father had turned all her young men friends away. Strong told her that his father had done the same, sending all his young lady friends away. The two talked quietly, as friends, and the evening passed quickly. As night fell, their hands touched. Then their lips touched. Soon their hearts touched, and they were in love.

Strong asked Red Flower to marry him and she agreed. They went up the pathway to the palace of the White King. Strong thought that his father could not object to his marrying a princess, but the king was angry that he had not been introduced to the princess before Strong proposed to her. The king refused to give his permission for Strong to marry Red Flower, and the prince became angry.

"I will leave this kingdom," he declared loudly, "and Red Flower and I will find happiness elsewhere."

Even though they had known each other only a short time, the prince and the princess were deeply in love. The two young lovers left Strong's home and went down to the beach in the moonlight. They climbed into the reed boat and Strong paddled them past the painted pole to the opposite shore.

In Red Flower's kingdom the two went to the palace to see her father. She thought that he could not possibly object to her marrying a prince; after all, who could be more suitable? But her father became angry at her for ignoring the customs of her people and accepting Strong's proposal before her family had approved. He told Strong to return to his own kingdom.

"If he must leave this place," said Red Flower boldly, "then I will also go." The two left, hand in hand, and walked back down the path to the Great Lake. There they sat on the edge of the reed boat and talked.

"Let us go to the Black Kingdom in the north," said Strong. "I am a friend of the prince there. I believe that they will welcome us."

So they paddled to the north, and when the moon was high they met with the Black King. He was kind to them, and Strong was pleased to see his friend the Black Prince, but the king told them firmly,

"This is a nation of warriors. Your fathers have forbidden you to marry. If I allow you to remain in my kingdom and to marry, either one of your fathers might make war on my kingdom. Worse, they might both attack at once, and divide my nation between them." Then he added softly, "That is what I would do." He paused for a moment. "You are both fine young people, and I admire your courage, but I must ask you to leave my kingdom."

Sadly, the young couple thanked the Black King. With an escort of warriors armed with clubs edged with sharp obsidian-glass blades, they returned to their reed boat. The warriors clasped Strong's hands in farewell, and Strong's friend, the Black Prince, gave Red Flower a kiss upon the cheek and gave Strong an embrace. Then the warriors pushed the young lovers' boat out into the lake.

"Let us go to the Blue Kingdom in the south," said Red Flower. "Their hospitality is great, and they will make us welcome." They paddled across the lake as the moon was setting and the stars were coming out. They reached the Blue Kingdom in the deep of night, but the guards at the palace greeted them most kindly, and awakened the Blue King. The king met them in the hallway of the palace, and touched their hands to his in welcome. They told him of their troubles.

"I value hospitality above all else," said the Blue King softly, "and you may rest here as long as you like. But I cannot allow you to marry and be prince and princess in my kingdom. What would my own children think? Sooner or later, they would become jealous of the hospitality you were receiving, because your presence here would make their positions as princes and princesses less important. No matter how good a host I might be, someday your welcome here would wear thin."

Strong and Red Flower thanked the Blue King for his kindness.

"We would not spend another minute in your home," said Strong, "knowing that it would someday lead to trouble for your children. We will go from this place."

The servants of the Blue King gave the two young lovers flowers, and food to eat in the boat. The king himself joined his servants and guards at the shore to wave farewell to Strong and Red Flower.

"Where will we go now?" asked Strong. "These four kingdoms are all the world that we know." He paused a moment in thought. "We could each go back to our own palaces, and never see each other again."

"I would rather not live than live without you," said Red Flower.

Strong smiled. He felt the same, and had hoped that Red Flower would say that.

"Let us go back to my kingdom," said the princess, "and go up the path to the place where I like to sit and think."

They pulled ashore in the Red Kingdom not long before dawn. Leaving the reed boat on the beach, they walked around a trail which bypassed the palace and wound on up the slope to the east. They reached the gap in the mountains and sat down to rest at the highest point. Red Flower was cold, so Strong built a small fire. As they sat warming themselves, Red Flower laid down to sleep. Strong covered her with his white feather cape. The smoke from the fire swirled around Strong as he sat quietly.

The clouds to the west rolled in over the lake until they stood beside the mountain pass in which the young lovers awaited the dawn. Out of the clouds came the great Aztec god, Feathered-Serpent. He came down from the sky and lay on the rocks, where he transformed himself into a man with a huge white feather headdress.

"Tépetl," said Feathered-Serpent-in-the-form-of-a-man, "This is the first night of your life that you have not come into my temple to burn incense. I was very worried about you, my dear friend."

Strong sighed, and greeted Feathered-Serpent, the god of the west. He explained how he and Red Flower had fallen in love, and now found themselves outcast by all the world that they knew.

"Great Feathered-Serpent," said Strong-like-the-Mountain, "could you make one of the kings change his heart and accept us into his kingdom as prince and princess?"

Feathered-Serpent-in-the-form-of-a-man sat and was silent for a moment. Then he spoke softly.

"I am sorry, Tépetl, but *I am only a god.* I cannot change what men and women feel in their hearts. Only men and women can do that for themselves."

Strong was silent for a moment.

"Then," he asked softly, "could you make it possible for Red Flower and me to be together forever?"

Feathered-Serpent smiled a sad smile. "Ah, Tépetl, my dear friend, that I can do."

Feathered-Serpent stood, and the feathers of his great white headdress stirred in the dawn breeze. The great serpent uncoiled into its true form. It raised its head up, up until it reached to the clouds, though its enormous tail still touched the earth. Then it pushed off, and its huge serpent body re–entered the clouds. Where the gap in the mountains had been, there now lay a huge new mountain, covered with a blanket of white snow. It looked like a woman lying on her side, covered with a white feather cape. The Aztecs later named it Ixtaccíhuatl *(Eesh-tahk-SEE-wahtl),* "The Reclining Woman." Beside it was a volcano that looked like a man kneeling down beside the woman, with volcanic smoke circling about him. The Aztecs called it Popocatépetl *(Poh-poh-kah-TEH-petl),* "The Smoking Mountain."

And there they sit, century after century, surely as happy as mountains can be. For the great Feathered-Serpent answered their prayer, and they are together, in love, forever.

In Texcoco:
Hungry Coyote's Lament

The Aztec city of Tenochtitlán was not the only capital city in or around the lake in the Valley of Mexico. Another city that was the capital of a small empire was Tlacopán (Tlah-coh-PAHN), west of the lakes. Still another capital was Texcoco (Tesh-KOH-koh), in the eastern side of the flat valley. These three cities, and the kingdoms of which they were the capitals, formed a triple union. The cities were friendly towards one another and so were their kings. Although there had been wars between the Indian kingdoms in the past, and there would be wars in the future between the Indians and the Spanish people, 1492 was a year of peace.

In Texcoco, the king was a man named Netzahualpilli (Nets-ah-wahl-PEEL-yee), which means "The Hungry Prince," referring to the old practice of going without food for a while in order to concentrate on important beliefs while forgetting the needs of the body. Hungry Prince's father, long dead by then, had been a great and wise king named Netzahualcóyotl (Nets-ah-wahl-KOH-yohtl), or "Hungry Coyote."

Hungry Coyote had also been a poet and musician. He wrote many fine poems that were learned by memory and sung by his people and the wise men of that time.

As the stars passed overhead on the night of October 12, 1492, Hungry Prince strolled in the flower garden of his royal palace in Texcoco. Even the bravest warriors among the Aztec people wore colorful feathers in their war crowns, and wore flowers on their shields and their heads when they went into battle.

Hungry Prince began to sing a song written by his father, a song about the Three Kingdoms and some of the kings who had ruled them, before Hungry Coyote died in 1472. It is a song about friendship because the chiefs of the Three Kingdoms were friends in Hungry Coyote's day. It is a sad song because Hungry Coyote was singing about death, and how death ends a friendship.

This is the song which the son of Hungry Coyote sang.

I want to sing for a moment,
Since I have a moment to spend,
May my song be enjoyed by you,
If it is worth it, my friend;
And so I begin my song's intent,
But more than a song, it's a sad lament.

Now, my friend, let us be glad,
And enjoy the flowers that bloom,
And forget the troubles we've had,
And forget all our fear and gloom,

And in this garden, my friend,
The sadness of life can end.

As I sing, I will play the music of life,
And dance in the garden a while,
And enjoy the works of the Powerful God.
Be happy in the glory of our belief,
For life as we live it on Earth is so brief.

From out of your own place you leave,
Into the court of this kingdom you come,
Onto the colorful cloth-covered throne.
Surely our empire shall enlarge, I believe,
And rise as the leader of the Earth all alone.

You are wise Oyoyotzín *(Oh-yoh-yoht-SEEN),*
Famous king and a monarch unique,
The garden of flowers you've seen,
Someday again you will seek.

Someday Fate will be cruel and devour
Your kingly wand, a symbol of power.
The beautiful moon of your glory will set,
And all of your servants abandon you yet.

And all of the princes who rise from your nest
Like eagles today, will someday fall.
As their noble fathers before them now rest
In the poverty of death, so shall they all.

All your great deeds will only be memories,
Your glories and victories all will be passed.
The joys of today will turn into tears
That flow to the ocean of darkness at last.

All of your royal family,
Who serve you with feathers and crown,
Will, after you leave this life and them,
Suffer loss, and their heads shall bow down.

And this unique greatness,
Our kingdoms enjoy with their crowns and their shield,
Will be worn down by Fate and Time,
And the three great thrones their might shall yield.

In nearby Aztec-Mexico, their famous king
Motecuhzoma the First, is one of three who reigned;
Hungry-Coyote of Texcoco, I who now sing,
Am the second ruler in this plain.
The third great king upon his throne
Is Totoquil *(Toh-toh-KEEL),* by luck alone.

I am not afraid the Earth will forget
The great deeds done in this wonderful place,
The Lord of the World, with His own hand
Made these things happen by His own grace.

Enjoy what you have now. And with flowers
From this garden of life make your crown.
Hear my song. Hear my music these hours;
I sing so you'll smile, and not frown.

Everything in this life is just borrowed.
It's not real, it will all pass away.
This is the great truth. This is the great question
That we all must answer someday.

Where are the kingdoms of days gone by?
Where are the flowery knights of the past?
Where are their voices, their deeds?
They rest with the dead at long last.

So, let us now, today,
Befriend one another and bind us together.
Nothing in this life is certain at all,
The future will bring change,

Like the change in the weather.

In Tlatelolco: Wailing Woman

The hour was late, the middle of the night approaching. Just outside the island city of Tenochtitlán, across a long earthen bridge called a causeway, lay the city of Tlatelolco (Tlah-teh-LOHL-koh). A group of boys who attended a sacred school there lay awake on their sleeping mats. (Theirs was a boarding school; they slept in the school buildings and only went home on feast days).

This is one of the scary Aztec stories they told.

Once there was a widow woman of low birth who was poor but very beautiful. Her husband had died falling off the causeway of Tlatelolco into the lake. He had been carrying a heavy load on a strap and it held him under until he drowned. The woman lived near the causeway and sold squash in the marketplace with her two little sons.

One day, the woman was sitting in the marketplace with her children when a handsome prince came along, carried on a traveling chair by four slaves. The prince saw the beautiful widow woman selling squash. He ordered his slaves to stop and set down his traveling chair, which was called a litter. He stood up, stepped off his litter, and went to the woman.

He bought some squash and asked her to deliver it to the palace where he lived, for he had no room on the litter to carry it.

When the woman went to the palace at sundown, the servants invited her in. The prince had planned it this way.

She soon fell in love with the prince and they met many times, but he never really loved her. He was only toying with her affection.

At last she told the prince that she wanted to marry him and become his princess. The prince did not want to marry her, but he did not know what to say. Then he had an idea.

The prince told her that he could not marry her because she had children, and they would become little princes if she became a princess. This would offend the rest of the royal family, he said, because they would accept only little princes of whom he was the father.

Knowing that the woman loved her sons and could never give them up, he felt this explanation would keep her from asking again.

The woman left that night, and as she was walking to her home she crossed the causeway where her husband had drowned. She stood for a long time looking into the dark water. At last she had made up her mind. She wanted to be a princess and, she thought, only her children stood in the way.

Back at the house, she woke the two boys and led them out to the causeway. They went to the spot where the boys' father had fallen in. She told her sons that the gods of the lake had asked them to come and live in the lake with their father.

Then the squash woman threw the two children into the lake, and they drowned. The two boys went to the Heaven of the Rain God, where they found their father and were happy. But the woman had been lying about the water gods. She had killed the children so that she could marry the prince.

The next day she went to the prince and told him that she could now marry him. She told him the children would no longer stand in their way, because she had drowned them in the waterway of reeds.

When the prince heard this he was horrified and disgusted by what she had done. She was an evil person, and he hated her. He would have had her killed for her crime, but he felt that it was his fault for lying to her about the marriage.

He turned the evil woman out, and told her never to come to his palace again. The prince went into the temple of his gods and prayed and burned sweet-smelling grass and asked for forgiveness.

The squash woman went crazy because of her crime. She began to wander the night, crying for her lost children. Finally she grew old and died and went to the Land of the Dead, but she did not find her children there for they were in the Heaven of the Rain God. She went to the Lord of the Dead, the Skeleton Man, and asked his permission to go back to the land of the living.

He was so tired of hearing her cry for her children that he let her go so that the dead could have some peace and quiet. She crossed back over the Flint Road to the land of the living, but all her flesh had rotted off or been cut away by the sharp flint on the road to and from the Land of the Dead.

She came back as a skeleton, her bones rotting and fleshless. She wore the same ragged, white cotton dress she had worn in life. She wandered all night along the causeways and beside the water, looking for her lost children.

Now she is like a goddess. She has powers. She can turn herself back into a beautiful woman and talk to you. But if you answer her, she will take your soul from you. You must avoid her like death itself. When she knows you cannot escape her, she turns from the beautiful squash woman into the skeleton she really is. She looks like the Lady of the Dead, the Skeleton Woman, wife of the Lord of the Dead.

But she is the One-Who-Cries-at-Night.

And she brings death.

Skeleton's Revenge

*The Aztec people had many of the same kinds of games as we have today. One of their games was called **patolli** (pah-TOH-lee). Because the game also had some religious importance, the game was outlawed by the Spanish after 1521. Only in this twentieth century did some Mexican Indians admit that they still play **patolli** in secret. Here is a scary story about a **patolli** game.*

A group of Aztec men sat together in a room, gambling on a reed mat. They played *patolli,* the game of beans given to the Aztecs by Five-Flower, the god of gambling. The men were so much in love with gambling that they bet more and more of their worldly goods with each game. An Aztec man might gamble away all his belongings, then bet his children and lose them, then bet his wife and lose her, and in one last attempt to win everything back, he would bet his own life into slavery. If he won, he got back all he had lost. If he lost, he had to become the slave of the winner, who could sell him in the slave market for silver, or gold, or trade goods.

Two men were the best players that night. One by one the other men had lost the colorful feathers from their warrior's hats, or the gold bracelets from their hands, or their nose-jewelry, or their ear-plugs. One by one they dropped out of the game and left, until only two men remained.

They gambled and gambled. One man, a tall, dark warrior, was winning everything. The other, shorter man was losing everything.

The loser lost his cotton shirt, his jewelry, and all his belongings. Then he lost his house, his children, and finally his wife. In one last try to win everything back he bet his life against it all.

He threw the beans in the air and clapped his hands, and called out the name of the god Five-Flower for good luck.

He lost.

Before he gave himself over to a lifetime of slavery, he told the winner of the *patolli* game that he wanted to go to a temple and pray for forgiveness for his foolishness. The tall man agreed, and said that they would meet on one of the streets nearby.

When the two left the room where they had played *patolli,* one went out to the street and the other went to a temple.

All the way to the temple, the loser was trying to think of something to do to win back his belongings. At the temple square there was a sacrificial stone, where a human sacrifice had been made. A flint knife still lay on the stone, covered with blood. It was not normal for a sacrificial knife to have been left behind.

The short man took this as a sign from the gods. He was to use the knife to get his belongings back. He took the knife and went back to the street where the tall man was waiting to take him into slavery. Since no one else had stayed at the game, only these two men knew who had won and who had lost.

The loser raised the knife high, and plunged it into the skull of the winner. The tall man fell dead.

The loser dragged the dead body down the street to a weedy place, and laid the body there for the dogs to eat. He tried to pull the sacrificial knife out of the skull of the dead man, but it would not come out, no matter how hard he pulled. This was an evil sign, but the loser left the knife in the skull of the body and went back to the street where he had committed his crime.

He went into the room where they had played *patolli,* and gathered all the winnings. He told his friends that with the last throws of the beans he had won everything from the tall man. At last, he said, the tall man had bet his own life in slavery against all the other belongings, and lost. When he had lost the last bet, the short man said to his friends, the tall stranger had run out into the night.

Since no one had seen the tall stranger in quite a while, everyone guessed he had run away to avoid becoming a slave.

The loser of the *patolli* game was wealthy now, with all the belongings of the dead man and all the other winnings from that terrible night. He became famous in the town of Tlatelolco, where he lived. He bragged about what a good gambler he was, and laughed at others who had lost their goods in games of *patolli*. He bought some slaves and was mean to them.

One night, the rich loser went for a long walk along the causeway near his home, close to the weedy place where he had laid the body on that night so long ago. It was a dark, starry night, and no one else was out walking at that hour.

Just then, the rich loser saw a tall man ahead of him.

The tall man was walking toward him.

The tall man was only a skeleton with all his flesh eaten away.

The tall man had a flint knife in his skull.

The tall man pulled the knife out of his skull with no effort at all.

The tall man took hold of the terrified little loser and drove the knife into his cowardly skull.

The next morning, people walking to market found the rich loser dead on the causeway, with a sacrificial flint knife in his skull. Lying on top of his dead body was a rotten skeleton, the bones all coming apart from one another.

Down the street, men gathered in a courtyard to play *patolli*.

On Board the Santa María

The flagship of the little fleet, as a group of ships is called, was the **Santa María.** *She—ships are always called "she"—was owned by Juan de la Cosa (HWAHN deh lah KOH-sah), a man from the northern part of Spain known as Galicia (Gah-LEE-see-ah). She had the new kind of rope rigging and canvas sails. In the centuries before, ships had had one large sail; now ships had several sails of different sizes, which made it easier to steer the ship by turning the sails to catch the wind in different ways. She was all wood, with very ornate carving for decoration. She was called by her true name, which means "Holy Mary" or "Saint Mary," instead of by her nickname, which was La Gallega (Lah Gahl-YEH-gah), meaning "the Lady from Galicia."*

It was well past the midnight hour now, and most of the Indian people of the New World were asleep. Aboard the **Santa María,** *only two or three sailors were still awake. One was the cabin boy who turned the hourglass.*

There were several cabin boys on each ship, and one stayed awake at all times to turn the only way of telling time, the hourglass.

Although the hourglass was needed most when sailing to help figure time and distance, it was turned every hour regardless of whether or not the ship was at anchor. As he watched the glass, waiting for the sand to run down into the lower bell, waiting until time to turn the glass, the cabin boy talked with an older sailor who walked the decks as a night watch.

The older man had memorized parts of the long story of El Cid, the famous knight of the crusade years in Spain. The story is a poem of thousands of lines and very few people knew the entire poem. But many men had learned to recite their favorite parts, handed down orally over the centuries.

Everyone knew the plot of the long story by heart, as they had heard it all many times before. But in a society where few people knew how to read, reciting and hearing favorite stories, songs, and poems over and over was always pleasant.

The Chests of Sand

Spain was divided into many tiny kingdoms in the eleventh century. Each kingdom had its own petty little king; some were Christians and some were Moslems. And in both kinds of kingdoms lived many Jews as well. Men and women were not measured by their religion, but by whether they were good or bad. Nevertheless, wars often broke out between the small kingdoms, and the fighting was usually between the Christians, who had lived in Spain for a thousand years, and the Moslems, whose ancestors had invaded Spain in the year 711, only three centuries earlier.

Rodrigo Díaz de Bivar (Roh-DREE-goh DEE-ahss deh Vee-VAHR) was a nobleman who owned land and a castle in northern Spain. He married a lovely lady named Ximena (Shee-MEH-nah). During fighting with neighboring Moslem kingdoms, whose inhabitants were called Moors, Rodrigo was knighted by the king of Castille. There was not yet a large nation named Spain. (That did not come until Ferdinand and Isabella's time.) Sir Rodrigo made the cities he had conquered pay him tribute, like taxes, as was the custom in those days. When the

Moorish cities sent their taxes, the men who brought the gold would kneel before Rodrigo and kiss his gloved hand as a sign of respect. When they talked to him, they called him by the Arabic title Sidi, which means "My Lord." When the king of Castille heard of this, he declared that everyone would call Sir Rodrigo by this Moslem title, which became, in Spanish, El Cid.

When the old king of Castille died, his will divided his kingdom into smaller pieces for his sons. This led to bitter hatred among the brothers, and violent civil war broke out as each brother tried to take all of his father's former land for himself. King Sancho and King Alfonso fought each other bitterly. When open battle failed, King Alfonso had his brother murdered—or so it has always been believed.

With King Sancho dead, King Alfonso tried to govern all the land that had been his father's, but El Cid refused to swear loyalty to him. Because he suspected King Alfonso of murdering King Sancho, El Cid became an enemy of King Alfonso. Alfonso banished El Cid from the kingdom, making him leave behind all his lands, his castle, and everything he had. El Cid, a brave and loyal knight under King Sancho, was treated like a traitor by King Alfonso.

The tale of "The Chests of Sand" begins as El Cid leaves his castle to go into exile. The poem rhymes in Old Spanish, but as we read it in English, the lines merely tell the story and only rhyme part of the time.

Tears fell from his eyes as he turned and looked back at his castle.

He saw the doors standing open, the gates unlocked, and the perches of his pet hunting birds empty and still. There were no fur blankets on the porches, and his hunting birds were gone. No falcons were left, not even a molted hawk.

My Lord El Cid gave a great sigh, and prayed about his sorrow. "Oh, Lord in Heaven, this is what my enemies at the court of the king have done to me."

He and his followers spurred their horses, and let loose their reins, and as they rode out of the castle of Bivar, they saw a crow flying on their right. As they rode toward the king's capital, the town of Burgos, they saw a crow flying on their left. This was a bad sign.

"Be merry," said My Lord to his friend, Álbar Fáñez *(AHL-bahr FAHN-yess)*. "We are in exile." And perhaps he added, "But we will return to the kingdom of Castille in glory in a while!"

My Lord Rodrigo Díaz entered the outskirts of the city of Burgos. His followers, his soldiers, carried their lances high, with pennants fluttering in the breeze: sixty pennants, sixty loyal men.

The men and women of Burgos leaned out the windows of their houses to look at the procession. Some cried, knowing how El Cid had been wronged. "What a loyal servant this man would be to his king, if only he had a good king to serve!"

The good people of Burgos would have invited him and his men into their homes and courtyards, but no one dared.

King Alfonso was so angry with El Cid that he had sent royal decrees out into the city with heavy wax seals of authority on them. The decrees warned that if anyone gave hospitality to El Cid, the host's belongings would be taken away, the host's eyes would be gouged out, the host would be killed, and the King would pray that the host's soul would never get to heaven as God willed.

These good Christian people of Burgos were sad, but no one dared say so.

El Cid, who had been the late king's champion, stopped at an inn to see if he and his men could get supper. The doors were locked tight. Unless someone broke them down they would not open. They were locked with bolts, both lower and upper.

El Cid's men called, but no one inside dared to answer. El Cid rode his horse to the door and knocked with his boot. The door remained closed.

Then a brave little girl came and spoke to El Cid.

"My champion, you put on your sword in a good hour,
But sealed letters of warning, sent by the king's power,
Hospitality to you and your men do forbid.
We cannot let you enter in any wise,
Or the cruel king will gouge out our eyes,
Take all our belongings and kill the host,
And send to sorrow each poor suffering ghost.
You would gain nothing by bringing us blindness.
Please leave, and God reward you for kindness!"

The girl hurried back to the inn, out of sight,
And El Cid knew that all she had told him was right.
He spurred his horse and turned back to the gate.
They rode out of the courtyard of the inn riding straight
For the Church of Holy Mary in Burgos, the city.
And there El Cid knelt down and prayed for pity.

On his horse once again, with his followers behind him,
Out the gates of the city he went.
Over the bridge of Arlanzón *(Ahr-lahn-SOHN),* to find
    him
A campsite in the fields where this night could be spent.
My Lord, El Cid, who in an hour that was good,
Put on his sword, spent the night in this wood.
His faithful soldiers encamped around.
But for prayers or money no food could be found.

In the city of Burgos lived one good man,
El Cid's kinsman, Martín Antolínez *(Mahr-TEEN Ahn-*
    toh-LEE-nehs), a fine
Soldier who brought El Cid bread and wine.
He carried it with him, it was his plan.
El Cid's soldiers ate too. The King had said
No one could sell El Cid supplies.
Martín didn't buy them. It was no surprise
Someone would bring out this wine and bread.

"This king will be angry if he finds out I've fed
My lonely kinsman," Martín then said.
There's only one thing left for me to do.
And that is escape and go with you.
Let's rest tonight, and go to church for morning prayers.
My life's not worth a fig if the king catches me un-
    awares.

In a good hour My Lord El Cid put on his sword.
He called Martín Antolínez, the brave lancer.
Martín was his kinsman, and quick to answer.
"I've no silver or gold nor can I afford

To pay you for all of your service and trouble,
But someday I promise your wages to double!
But now, I must do something that I know to be wrong.
I need your help, these are my requests:
Build me two great wooden chests,
They must be heavy and very strong.
Decorate them with leather that is tooled in design.
Paint the leather bright red, and make it look grand.
To make the chests heavier, fill them with sand.
Decorate the chests with nail-studs, gold-covered and
    fine."

El Cid explained, "In Burgos, inside the city wall,
Live two fine moneylenders, named Vidas *(VEE-dthas)*
    and Raquel *(Rah-KEHL)*.
They are honest men and I know them well.
Tonight, in secret you must pay them a call.
Tell them their friend El Cid has been exiled,
He has chests of treasure too heavy to carry.
He wants to pawn them. The money is very
Important to him as he camps in the wild.
Go in darkness so that no Christian can know
What you do, and may God show you care.
You know I would not otherwise dare
To do this wrong thing, but I must. Now go!"

Martín rode to the gates and inside the city wall
And on Sir Raquel and Sir Vidas paid a call.
These men were quietly counting their gold,
They had earned from pawn and things they had sold.
Martín arrived to strike a deal.
"Dear Sirs, you know that our friendship is real.

I must talk with you in secret about a pawn."
And quickly the three to a private room were
    withdrawn.
The men all shook hands as friends should.
"I can make you both rich for good,"
Martín said, "but no Christian nor Moor
Must know of our plan. My Lord, El Cid,
Has tribute from his conquered cities hid
In two great chests. You'll never be poor,
For this treasure El Cid has kept
From before the king made him leave his land.
There's pure gold inside. (He lied; it was sand!)
And we will pawn the treasure to you...except
When we turn the chests over to you to keep
In your safe room, you must promise at last
Not to open the chests 'til a year has passed."

Sir Raquel and Sir Vidas their profits reap
From their business deals, and they agree
To accept the chests 'til El Cid should return.
If he never comes back, the treasure they'll earn.
If he pays them back the pawning fee,
He'll pay them interest. "Bring the treasure,"
They tell Martín. "And now, what fee
For El Cid and for you shall we agree?"
"Six hundred marks of silver shall you measure,"
Replied Martín. "We will pay you, with pleasure,"
Said Raquel and Vidas. "But first you must bring
The chests to us, before anything
Is paid to you to pawn this treasure."

Together Martín and his Jewish friends alone
Bypassing the bridge over the Arlanzón,
Crossed the stream by water so that no one would know
In all Burgos where the three would go.
At the tent of El Cid, they dismounted and entered.
Sir Raquel and Sir Vidas kissed El Cid's hand,
The same as the servants in My Lord's old land.
El Cid smiled and greeted them kindly and centered
Their attention on this: "You will never be poor
As long as you live. I am in exile and you
Shall have keep of my treasure in chests: these two!"
Martín then gave the terms. "You know you're
To keep the chests safe, but also you swear
Not to open them up while they're in your care,
Until a year has passed. You have promised both
To pay six hundred silver marks and to keep your oath."

They all agreed on the terms. The chests were sent
With Sirs Raquel and Vidas down the road.
"We must leave this wood before the rooster has
        crowed,"
Martín warned the two pawnbrokers, before off they
        went.
The chests were so heavy they could hardly be moved.
"Our Lord," said the Sirs, "in a good hour indeed
You put on your sword. We're your friends in need.
May your conquests in foreign lands be approved.
May we give you this fine robe of Moorish red!
We kiss your glove in farewell," they then said.

"It pleases me," said El Cid, with his last requests:
"Carry the treasure. Count the pawn money out on the
    chests!"
In the secrecy of a private chamber the money was
    counted.
On a clean white bedsheet and carpet the coins were
    thrown.
Five strong soldiers had carried the chests and looked
    on.
And three hundred silver marks the fee amounted.
Then the gentlemen added the three hundred more
In marks of gold from their golden store.
The five men loaded the money and departed.

The three friends spoke before Martín started.
"I deserve a fee," said Martín, "for bringing this treasure
To you, which can make you rich beyond measure."
"We will give thirty marks," agreed the two men.
"And a fine cloak and also a warm fur skin."
Martín gave them thanks and left on the ride
And recrossed the river, and came to the wood
Where the tent of My Lord El Cid stood.
El Cid received him with open arms inside.

El Cid and the Lion

The watchman made a round of the decks and came back.
While he was gone, it came time to turn the glass. The boy
turned the glass, sang a little song, and said a prayer. The
watchman in the forecastle high above him said, "Amen."

The watchman came back on deck.

"Now," he said, "you tell me a legend of El Cid."

"I don't know the poetry," said the boy. "Only the
story."

And he told of the time El Cid's lion was let loose.

El Cid was a great hero, after conquering the city of
Valencia. He was offered the crown of a king to rule
over Valencia, but he gave the crown to the king of
Castille, and was allowed to return to his home and lands.
But now, of his two daughters: the two grown girls
married two young noblemen from the lands of Carrión
(Kah-ree-OHN). These young men were handsome, but
lazy, and El Cid grew impatient with them.

It came to pass one day that El Cid was at his supper.
All his loyal men dined with him and his sons-in-law, also.

After supper it was El Cid's custom, as he was now getting old, to give his orders and make a speech, and then to nap for a while upon the great throne. Later he would awaken, rested, and join the men who were playing the game of tables, or the game of chess, to pass the evening.

Now El Cid had dined and spoken and was about to nap, when a messenger came with the news that a great Moorish king, Búcar *(BOO-kahr),* was sailing with a fleet of ships to attack the coast of Spain at Valencia. El Cid was pleased at the thought of going into battle again, but he took his nap all the same.

Now El Cid had a pet lion which he had kept for many a year, and it had grown strong. Three men were in charge of this lion, to feed it and clean its cage. The cage was well inside the palace of the Alcázar *(Ahl-KAH-sahr),* in a courtyard. The men who had charge of the lion were cleaning the courtyard when they heard the rumor that an army of Moors was coming. In fear and panic, they came to the hall where El Cid was napping, but they foolishly forgot to close the gate to the lion's courtyard.

After the lion had eaten his supper, he saw the open gate and came down into the palace, to the supper-hall where El Cid was sleeping and the other men were playing at tables and at chess, which are games of war.

As the curious lion walked slowly into the hall, the soldiers were startled, but the young lords of Carrión were very cowardly! One son-in-law jumped out a window and landed in a wine press full of sour grapes, and smelled of sour grapes all night after that. The other son-in-law ran and hid under El Cid's throne.

The soldiers of El Cid were too busy to laugh just then. They wrapped their cloaks around their arms, in case the lion should bite them, and then they drew their swords and stood in a circle around El Cid's throne to protect him.

The nobles of Carrión made such a noise hiding and jumping out the window that they woke El Cid!

He saw the lion and calmly got down off the throne. He walked to the lion and spoke to the great beast. He took it by the fur of its mane as if it were a gentle dog, and led it back to its cage.

First, everyone was amazed at how calm and brave El Cid was. Then they all laughed at how foolish and cowardly the nobles of Carrión had been.

The cabin boy and the night watch laughed together. Then the cabin boy looked concerned, and he added:

But it went badly after that, for the sons-in-law grew to hate El Cid and mistreated his daughters thereafter.

Then all was ended well when the nobles of Carrión were declared traitors by the king.

The night watch smiled. Of course, he knew that was how that story ended, but the boy felt he had to tell that part, too.

*As the **Santa María** rocked slowly in the waves, the watchman went off on another round. The cabin boy looked out across the dark waters to the south, wondering if China were that way—or if that were the way to Japan.*

He could not know yet that Asia was very far away, and to the south lay a great continent that would someday be called South America.

On the Mainland of South America

On the northern coast of South America, on the shores and deeper inland in the jungles, lived a tribe of Indians known as the Carib (Kah-REEB). Their name would eventually be given to the sea between the islands visited by Columbus and the mainland of South America. It would be called the Caribbean.

Columbus would see these Carib people living on islands in the Caribbean and on its shores when he sailed back to the New World on his fourth voyage.

The Caribs were the enemies of the Taino people on the island of Guanahaní, where the **Niña, Pinta** and **Santa María** were now anchored.

The Tree of Life

Some of the Carib people sat around a fire at midnight, acting as night watch for their village. The Carib were warlike people and had to protect themselves from their enemies.

As they sat before the fire, one of the older Carib tribesman began to tell a story from the inland jungles, the story of the Creator God Makunaima (Mah-koo-NIGH-mah) and the Tree of Life.

In the beginning of the Forest World, the Carib people had very little to eat. (They had not yet learned to plant the cassava roots.) The animals and birds also had very little to eat. Everyone was hungry.

But one little animal, the agouti *(ah-GOO-tee)*, a large forest rodent, seemed sleek and fat and healthy. He went out every morning, far away into the forest. When he came back in the evening he seemed to have eaten. He dropped banana skins, cane strips, and other things the people and animals had never seen.

The people and animals called a council and spoke to each other. They decided that the little agouti must have found a place where there was food to eat.

They decided to send one animal to follow the agouti when he went out the next morning, to see where he went, and come back and tell the rest of them. The first day, they sent the snake.

The snake waited for the agouti to pass on his morning journey, and then he followed the little rodent a long, long way into the forest. The snake saw the agouti stop and look back to see if anyone was following him. The snake became afraid that he had been seen or heard rustling among the leaves. He stayed behind, and the agouti went on. The snake had nothing to report, but the agouti came back looking well-fed again that evening.

The next morning the people and animals selected the woodpecker to fly above the forest floor and watch the agouti from above. The agouti looked around and did not see or hear anything following him on the ground. But the woodpecker saw some bugs in the bark of a tall tree, and he could not help but peck on the bark a little bit to get some of the bugs to eat. The agouti heard the woodpecker and suspected he was being followed, so he picked up some bitter weeds and pretended to chew them as if they were what he ate.

The woodpecker reported back to the people and animals. They tasted the bitter weeds and knew they had been fooled.

The next day the people and the animals sent the rat to follow the agouti. Brother rat is the most sneaky and quiet of all the animals. He has to hide from people and meat-eaters all the time, and he can move more quietly than anyone.

The agouti never knew the rat was following him. He stopped and looked all around and listened high and low, and when he could not hear or see anyone following him, he went to his secret place.

Brother rat followed.

The agouti went to the tallest tree in the forest and gathered all manner of fruit from the ground underneath the tree. It was a most wonderful tree! Every fruit grew on its branches: bananas, plums, mangos, papayas. Every good root grew at the foot of the tree: cassava, yuca, yams. Every good berry and bean grew under its leaves, and every good grass and grain grew from its bark.

As soon as the agouti had eaten his fill, he wiped his face with his paws and went away.

The rat came back and told the people and the animals what he had seen. They all went back to the tree, led by the rat. By the time they reached the tree, many ripe fruits and other good things had fallen to the ground. They picked these up and ate them. After everyone was full, they talked about how to get more fruits and food down. No one could climb the tree; it was too big and the bark was too smooth.

After much talking, they decided to cut the tree down so they could reach all the fruit and berries and food growing on it, and dig up all its good roots to eat.

The people and the animals went and got stone axes and began to cut. They cut for ten days, but the tree would not fall. They cut for another ten days, and still the tree would not fall. By now they were very hungry again, and very thirsty.

The people got calabash gourds off the lower parts of the tree and cut them open to make water-carriers. Each animal was given a gourd to carry water in, so everyone would have something to drink while they worked.

But the agouti, who had come upon them cutting the tree on the second day, was sternly punished for being so greedy and keeping the tree to himself. Everyone scolded him, especially the monkey, who scolds so much even today. When all the animals were given gourds to carry water in, they gave the agouti a basket woven of grass so he couldn't get much water, as a punishment.

After ten more days of cutting, the tree fell at last.

The people took away as their share what they plant today: cassava, cane, yams, bananas, potatoes, pumpkins and watermelons. The animals took what they wanted: the birds took seeds, the rodents took grains, some of the others wanted green leaves, and so on.

The agouti was just getting back from the river, carrying his grass basket without much water left in it. When he got back only one kind of fruit was left. No one had taken the plums, so they became the food of the agouti.

This was the story about the Tree of Life, sent by Makunaima to feed his people and his animals, and about how the little agouti led the people and the animals to the Tree of Life.

On the Coast
of Portugal

The people of Europe counted the hours beginning at high noon each day, and the twelfth hour was midnight. The Indian people never counted the hours; time was of little importance to their way of life.

*The sun had set at what the Europeans would have called the sixth hour. As the sailors aboard the **Pinta** told of Don Juan, it was the seventh hour. As the Taino people told of the inaja-palm cave it was the eighth hour.*

*As the crew of the **Niña** told animal fables, it was the ninth hour. As the girls in the Aztec palace heard of the Smoking Mountain, it was the tenth hour. King Hungry Prince of Texcoco walked in his garden at the eleventh hour. The boys in Tlatelolco told their stories at the midnight hour.*

*The night watch on the **Santa María** told of El Cid in the first hour after midnight. The guards around the fire in the coastal village of the Carib people told of the Tree of Life at the second hour after midnight.*

As the people of the New World were going to sleep, the sun was about to come up in the Old World, in the home countries of Columbus's crew.

At the second hour after midnight in the Carib village, it was the sixth hour after midnight in the seacoast towns of Portugal, and the sun was about to rise.

Along the Atlantic coast of the small kingdom of Portugal lay many small villages and towns. Most of the families in these villages made their living from the sea. Some sailed on ships that traveled the world. Other families sent their fathers and brothers and sons out to fish for a living. In these families, the women and girls sewed the clothes for the fishermen, prepared their meals, and helped clean and dry the fish, or wove warm clothing to protect sailors from the cold winds at sea.

Men and boys repaired their fishing boats, tied cord into fishing nets and repaired the nets when they broke, and sewed the canvas sails. Before going out to fish at dawn, each small fishing boat had to be made ready. In the pre-dawn darkness, men sat tying new knots and repairing the fishing nets for the day's catch.

As they worked on their nets, they took turns telling stories.

The Iron Dancing Shoes

This story is very old, and was told all over Europe with many different names and many different endings. It was always the dream of a common boy to grow up and marry a princess. It is the boy's politeness and intelligence that allow him to earn his magic helpers, commonly found in this kind of story.

One day long ago, the princess came to her father the king and asked for new dancing shoes. The king became angry because he had to order new shoes for her every day, and the royal shoemakers could hardly keep up with the demand. Thinking he could solve the problem, the king ordered that seven fine pairs of dancing shoes be made, but that they be made from iron so they would never wear out.

The royal shoemakers and the royal blacksmiths worked together and made the finest dancing shoes ever. They were decorated with silver and gold, and lined with silk. But their soles were made of iron, to last forever.

Sure enough, the next day the princess came back and wanted new shoes. She showed the old shoes, and their iron soles were worn completely through!

The king ordered more iron shoes to be made. But secretly he wondered what the princess was doing to wear out shoes so fast. He gave his advisors a secret decree, stating that any man who could discover how the princess wore out those shoes could marry the princess and become a prince.

That very same day, a sailor from Portugal came through the royal city. There he saw two foolish men hitting each other over and over again.

"Why are you two hitting each other?" asked the sailor.

"We are fighting over a cap," said one of the men, and he hit the other.

"If it means so much to you," said the sailor, "you may also take my cap, so that each of you may have one."

The two men stopped fighting. "No, no," said the other. "We must have this cap." He held up a bright red and green cap with a bell on its point. "This is a magic cap. When our father, the magician, died, he left this cap to whichever son is the smarter of the two of us."

"What does the magic cap do?" asked the sailor.

"If the wearer says, 'Cap, cap, cover me up,' the wearer becomes invisible," answered the other.

"I have an idea," said the sailor. "I will take this orange from my sack and throw it a great distance. Whoever reaches the orange first and brings it back to me, to him I will give the cap."

The foolish men agreed and handed the cap to the sailor. He threw an orange as far as he could, and the two men ran off after it.

"Neither of you is smarter than the other," said the sailor, "or you would not fall for such a simple trick." With that he put on the cap and said, "Cap, cap, cover me up!"

When the two men came back, fighting over the orange, the sailor was nowhere to be seen.

A little further down the road the sailor took the cap off and the world could see him again.

Now the sailor saw two men fighting over a pair of boots.

"This is a most curious town," said the sailor as he walked up to the men. "Tell me why you are fighting."

"We are fighting over this pair of boots," said one man, as he hit the other.

"If it means so much to you, I will gladly give you my boots and I will go barefoot so you may each have boots to wear."

"No, no," said one of the men. "These boots are special. Our father brought them from the Orient. In these boots a man may travel seven long leagues of land in the twinkling of an eye. The wearer has only to say, 'Boots, boots, run like the wind,' and he is gone. Our father promised them to whomever of us is the swiftest."

"Then I have a plan," said the sailor. "I will take an orange from my pack and throw it as far as I can. To whomever reaches the orange first and brings it back to me, I will give the boots."

The men agreed and handed the boots to the sailor. He took an orange out of his sack and threw it as far as he could. While the men ran off after the orange, the sailor put on the boots and said, "Boots, boots, run like the wind."

In the twinkling of an eye, the sailor was seven leagues away. The two men ran back, quarrelling over the orange, and found him gone.

The sailor was now almost out of the town on the other side, so he turned back toward the town square and walked at a normal pace.

On the way back to the square, he saw a large crowd gathered around the steps of the cathedral. The princess had worn out so many pairs of shoes, night after night, that the king had decided to make his secret decree public, and it was being read aloud to the people of the town. The sailor heard the promise that whoever solved the mystery could marry the princess, and he decided to give it a try.

The sailor went to the palace of the king, eating an orange out of his sack. When he was let in to see the king, he asked for the king's permission to solve the mystery.

"You are only a simple sailor," said the king. "You are not a wise man nor a magician. How can you solve the mystery of the seven pairs of iron dancing shoes?"

"I ask only that you let me give it a try," replied the sailor.

"Very well," said the king, a little angry. "But if you cannot find the answer to this puzzle after three days, I will have you put to death!"

The sailor bowed low before the king and accepted the terms. The king had thought the sailor would not take the risk, but it was too late now. The sailor had to be given a chance to try.

The sailor was dressed in a captain's suit, and seated at the supper table with the royal family. That night, he slept outside the princess's door.

As he was falling asleep, the princess opened her door and offered the sailor a drink of water. He was thirsty, so he thanked her and drained the cup. She smiled and went back in, closing her door. When the sailor awoke the next morning, he knew the drink had contained a sleeping potion. The princess opened the door and walked out, carrying seven pairs of worn-out iron shoes.

At the breakfast table, the king asked what the sailor had learned. When the sailor admitted he had learned nothing, the king said, "Two more days, and you die!"

That night the sailor slept inside the door of the princess's bedchamber and he did not take the drink when she offered it. But as he was falling asleep, the princess sprinkled a magic powder on him. When he woke up, he knew he had been tricked again. The princess walked past him to the door, carrying seven pairs of worn-out iron shoes.

At breakfast, the king asked again what the sailor had learned. Again, he replied he had learned nothing. "One more day, and you die!" said the king.

On the third night, the sailor slept on the floor beside the princess's bed, and he would not take the drink she offered, and he kept his eyes open so that she could not sprinkle magic powder over him.

"You have won," said the princess, and she pretended to go to sleep. The sailor also pretended to go to sleep on the carpet. The princess got up and walked toward the door with her seven new pairs of iron dancing shoes.

The sailor pulled the magic cap from under his coat and put it on. "Cap, cap," he whispered, "cover me up!"

As the princess went out the door, the sailor followed, but she could not see him. She went down the stairs and out the front door of the royal palace, with the sailor behind her. She got into a beautiful royal coach pulled by six white horses. As the coach sped away, the sailor said to his new boots, "Boots, boots, run like the wind!" and he ran off as fast as the coach and horses were going.

He followed the coach to the seashore, where the princess stepped out of the coach and walked to a pier. Docked at the pier was a fine ship with flags of many colors blowing in the breeze. The princess walked up the plank and onto the beautiful ship. The invisible sailor followed. The wind suddenly began to blow very strongly out to sea. The sails of the magic ship filled with wind, and the ship slid silently out from the pier and sailed faster and faster over the waves until it came to the Land of the Giants. There the wind laid low, and the ship glided up to a pier beside the castle of the king of the giants.

The princess left the ship and the invisible sailor followed.

At the gate of the castle a guard called out, "Who goes there?"

The princess answered, "The Princess of the Land of Harmony."

The guard answered, "You may both pass."

As the princess went through the gate, she looked back to see who else the guard was speaking to, but she saw no one.

At the door to the castle, another guard called out, "Who goes there?"

The princess answered, "The Princess of the Land of Harmony."

The guard stepped aside and opened the door for the princess. "You may both pass," he said.

The princess looked back to see who "both" could mean. She saw no one.

At the entryway to the Great Hall of the Giants another guard called out, "Who goes there?"

"The Princess of the Land of Harmony."

"You may both pass."

The princess thought these guards must have lost their minds, for she could see no one following her. But this was a magic land, and who could say what was happening?

Fearing that the giants could see him, the sailor hid under a great big chair in the Great Hall. The princess went to the prince of the giants, and they joined hands and began to dance as the giants' band played beautiful but very loud music.

The sailor watched as the princess danced for an hour, so fast that she wore out a pair of iron shoes. She took off the old shoes and put on a new pair, and she and the handsome giant began to dance again.

Seven hours and seven pairs of shoes later, the sun was about to come up. The guards entered to announce sunrise, and the princess gathered her worn-out shoes to take them home.

As she prepared to leave, the guards asked, "Where is your manservant?"

"What manservant?" asked the princess.

"The one who came in with you!" answered the three guards.

"FIND THIS MAN!" roared the prince of the giants.

The giants' wise man came into the room with a Book of Fate, which told everything there is to know about everyone and what their fate will be. He opened the book and began to turn the pages, looking for the page that would tell him where the sailor was hiding.

"Boots, boots," said the sailor, "run like the wind."

The sailor ran past the wise man, grabbed the Book of Fate, and ran out the door, knocking over all the furniture. The guards and the giants all ran after him, but no one could catch him. The sun was almost coming up when the princess ran onto the magic ship. No one could find the sailor, who was already hiding in the ship, and she couldn't see him either.

The wind took the ship back to the mainland, and the carriage took the princess back to the palace. The magic boots outran the carriage, and when the princess came into her bedchamber, there was the sailor, asleep on the carpet.

At breakfast, the king asked what the sailor had learned.

The sailor smiled and said, "I saw nothing unusual last night." (And considering what he had seen when he first came to this town, his answer was the truth!)

"Then today you die!" said the king. And soon...

The king's guards and the royal court had gathered in the courtyard. The royal headsman was standing by with his axe, ready to chop off the sailor's head.

"Do you have any last words?" asked the king.

"I would like to ask the princess a question," said the sailor.

"Ask whatever you like," said the king, impatiently.

"Did My Lady leave her bedchamber last night?" asked the sailor.

"No," said the princess, lying defiantly.

"Did My Lady ride in a carriage to the sea?"

"No!"

"Did My Lady sail in a magic ship to the Land of the Giants?"

"No!"

"Did My Lady dance with the prince of the giants in the Great Hall of the giants' castle?"

"No."

"And did the guards suspect that someone had followed My Lady?"

"No."

"And did the wise man of the giants bring forth the Book of Fate to find the manservant who followed you?"

The princess did not answer as quickly this time.

"No…"

The sailor pulled the Book of Fate from inside his coat.

"And is this not that book?"

The princess bowed her head.

"…Yes."

The king shouted with delight that the mystery had been solved. The royal court cheered. The headsman said nothing.

The sailor opened the Book of Fate and read aloud:

"And the sailor married the princess, and they lived happily all their days."

The Three Citrons of Love

As the people of Europe went forth to sail the seas and explore new lands, they often found strange new people and new foods. It is no wonder that they told stories about amazing people and wonderful fruits...like the three citrons of love.

Once there was a king of another land whose only son was very fond of hunting in the forest. As he went hunting one day, he met an old woman who looked as if she were starving. The prince never carried silver or gold when he went hunting, but his servants always brought along a large basket of food to eat at midday deep in the forest. The prince took pity on the old woman and called to his servants to bring the food basket. The servants spread out a cloth upon the grass and served a fine feast of mutton and bread and fruits and wine. He asked the old woman to sit down and join him in his midday meal.

The old woman ate and drank her fill, and thanked the kind prince. "I have nothing to give you in return for your kindness," she said. "but I do have these three citrons."

(Now, citrons are a small fruit like a lime, too sour to eat by themselves.)

The prince smiled, thinking the gift to be rather worthless, but his heart was touched that this poor woman should want to reward him. He took the three little citrons and bowed low in respect to the old woman.

As the servants packed the basket again, the old woman took her leave of the prince.

Her final words were, "When you cut open one of the citrons, cut lengthwise, not across the center. And always open the citrons only when you are beside a stream or fountain." Then the woman was gone.

The prince thought this was most strange, but he put the citrons in his hunting bag and went on his way.

After he had hunted for a few hours without finding any deer, the prince sat alone on a rock and decided to cut open a citron and enjoy its tart taste. He took out his skinning knife and one of the citrons. Forgetting what the old woman had said, he cut the citron open across its middle. Blood poured from the tiny fruit!

The prince let out a scream and jumped up. The fruit fell to the ground and looked for all the world like a normal citron, but the prince's hands were wet with blood.

The prince dried his hands on a kerchief and took out another citron. He cut it very carefully, as the woman had told him to, lengthwise. As he pulled the two halves apart, a small, beautiful young woman stepped out of the citron and grew to full size while standing before him.

"I am very thirsty," she said, for the taste of a citron is sour and makes the eater thirsty. "Give me a drink or I will die."

The prince had forgotten the second thing the old woman had told him. He was not near a stream or fountain, and had no water to give the lovely young woman.

The beautiful lady saw that the prince had no water. She fell to the ground and died, and withered like a dried fruit until there was nothing left of her but dust. The prince wept a tear for his own forgetfulness, and was very sad at the death of this magical maiden.

The prince then hurried to his palace and ran to the fountain in his private garden. There he sat down and opened the third citron.

Out stepped a small, beautiful woman, and she grew to full size before him.

"I am very thirsty," said the maiden. "Give me a drink or I will die."

The prince knelt at the fountain and lifted a handful of cool water, then another, then another. The maiden drank thirstily, and kissed his hand each time he brought it to her lovely lips.

The prince and the maiden spoke for hours, and he fell in love with her. They climbed up into a tree with low branches in the garden and sat there, talking. The prince asked the maiden to wait while he went to do his princely chores, but he advised her to stay in the tree in the garden, so that no one else would see her and ask who she was.

While the prince was gone and the maiden sat in the tree, an ugly old serving woman came out to draw water from the prince's fountain. Now, this old woman was evil and she practiced black magic, but she was allowed to scrub the floors in the palace, for no one knew she was a witch. She had been forbidden to draw water from the prince's private garden fountain, but she had come anyway, opening the locked gate by witchcraft.

As the old woman lowered her jar into the water, she looked into the fountain and saw the reflection of the beautiful maiden in the tree above her. She thought it was her own reflection!

"Well, Witch Weed," she said to herself, "this must be a magic pool that makes you so lovely." And she admired herself, turning her head this way and that.

The maiden in the tree saw what the witch was doing and began to laugh. Being the daughter of a good witch herself, the maiden immediately recognized this old woman as a bad witch.

Witch Weed looked around to see who was laughing and saw the maiden in the tree. "Come down, my pretty," she said, "and let me wash your lovely hair."

At first the maiden refused, but the witch threw magic dust at her, and she came down to the fountain after all. There the witch began to wash the maiden's long hair, asking polite questions about the prince, which the maiden answered. When the witch knew all she needed to know, she pulled out a long hairpin from her robe. She stuck the hairpin into the poor maiden's head! But it did not kill her. The hairpin was magic and changed the maiden into a beautiful white dove, which flew away into the sky.

The witch climbed the tree and sat where the maiden had sat.

The prince returned and was disgusted to see an old woman (whom he did not recognize as the old maid who scrubbed the floors) sitting where he had left the lovely maiden.

"What has happened?" asked the princc, almost in tears.

"I am bewitched," said the old woman. "I am lovely some of the time, and ugly the rest."

The prince believed the old woman and took her in. They lived together in the palace, but the witch never got any prettier.

One day the prince was walking in the garden, and a beautiful white dove flew down and landed on the tree where the maiden had sat days before. The dove spoke, as if by magic.

"Gardener of my garden," said the bird, "how goes it with the prince and his ugly lady?"

"We are content," answered the prince, still believing the witch to be the maiden he had loved.

The dove flew away.

The next day the prince went walking in the garden at the same hour hoping to see the magic dove again. She flew in and perched on the limb.

"If the prince and his lady are content," said the dove, "then is there no hope for me?"

The dove flew away.

The next day the prince made a bird snare of pretty ribbon to catch the dove. When he set the snare on the limb of the tree, the dove flew in but did not land.

"No snare of ribbon was meant for me," she said, and off she flew.

The next day he set a snare of silver cord.

"No snare of silver was meant for me," said the dove, and off she flew.

The next day he set a snare of tiny golden chain.

"No snare of gold was ever meant for me," she said, and off she flew.

The next day he thought of the maiden, and he cut open a citron and left it on the branch where the maiden had once sat. The dove flew in and sat on the branch, and drank the tart juice of the citron.

"I am very thirsty," said the dove. "Give me a drink or I will die."

Then the prince knew who the dove was. He took her in his hands, carried her to the fountain, and gave her a drink from his hand. As he lovingly petted the dove's beautiful head he found a hairpin stuck into her skull. He pulled the pin out, and the dove changed and grew into the beautiful citron maiden.

The prince ordered Witch Weed killed. He made a drum of her skin, and with her long bones he beat on the drum while everyone danced at the wedding of the prince and the citron maiden.

The Tower of Ill Fortune

Sometimes the brave sailors and explorers from Europe never returned from their travels, having died in a storm at sea, or been killed by the people of foreign lands. It is no wonder that scary stories were told about the dangers of traveling far from home.

There was a young hunter who had a fine horse, and one day he killed a lioness. The hunter had not seen the lioness's cub, or he would not have killed the mother. The huntsman regretted killing the lioness and took the cub to raise as his own. Soon the cub grew to be a fine young lion. He hunted with the huntsman as well as the finest hunting dog.

One day, as the hunter and his lion rode down the narrow roadway in the high mountains, they passed a woman washing clothes in a stream beside the road.

"Greetings, Auntie. What are you doing?" asked the young huntsman.

"Washing clothes here," she replied, "and I shall continue to do so all my life."

Seeing a tower of stone high on the hilltop, he asked, "What is the name of that fine castle tower?"

"Oh, child," said the woman, "that is the Tower of Ill Fortune. Whoever goes there never returns!"

"I shall go there," said the huntsman, foolishly, "and shall return here and find you washing still."

He rode to the tower and found that it had been turned from a watchtower into an inn. He knocked on the door, and an old man opened it. The huntsman asked for a room for the night. The old innkeeper gave him the huge key to the stables, and told him to open it for his horse and lion. But to keep the lion from eating anyone else's horse, the innkeeper gave the hunter a braid of hair, like a rope.

"Tie this hair braid around the necks of your horse and lion, and then tie them in the same stable stall."

The boy tied the horse and the lion in the stable, locked the door, and returned with the key. Inside the inn, he asked for supper. Suddenly the old innkeeper turned mean.

"You'll have to fight me for it!"

They began to fight, but the innkeeper was an evil magician and he quickly overpowered the young hunter.

"Come, Horse," called the youth. "Come, Lion! Come and help me!"

But the magician called, "Braid of hair, grow thick! Hold the horse and lion by this trick!"

The braid rope grew until it was heavy and strong, and the lion and the horse could not come to help their master.

The magician won the contest, and he put the hunter under a spell that turned the youth hard like stone. He stood the youth up like a statue in his hall, where animal heads and other trophies hung on the wall.

The younger brother of the hunter soon missed his older brother, and went out with his horse and hunting dog to look for the young huntsman. Soon, high in the mountains, he came to the woman washing clothes.

"Greetings, Auntie. What are you doing?" called the younger brother.

"Washing clothes here, and I shall continue to do so all my life."

"What tower is that, high on the hill?"

"Oh, child, do not go there. That is the Tower of Ill Fortune. Whoever goes there never returns."

"I shall go there, and return, and find you washing clothes still."

The younger brother rode up to the inn and knocked on the door. He asked for a room for the night. The innkeeper gave him the key and a braid of hair like a rope, and sent the boy to the stable with his horse and dog. There the boy saw the horse and lion of his older brother. He did as the innkeeper had told him, and went back into the inn.

Giving the key to the old man, he said, "Where is my brother, whose horse and lion are in the stable?"

"You'll have to fight me to find out!"

They began to fight and the boy called out, "Come, Horse! Come, Dog! Come and help me!"

But the magician said, "Braid of hair, grow thick! Hold the horse and dog by this trick!"

The hair braid grew so thick and heavy that the animals could not go to the aid of their master.

Soon the second brother was cold as stone and standing like a statue in the trophy hall.

Not long afterwards, the youngest brother missed his two older brothers and set out on his horse to find his brothers, carrying his pet cat along with him. Soon he came to the woman washing clothes up in the mountains.

"Greetings, Auntie. What are you doing?"

"Washing clothes here, and I shall continue to do so all my life."

"What is that tower on yonder hill?"

"Oh, child, that is the Tower of Ill Fortune. Whoever goes there does not return."

"I shall go there and return, and find you here washing still."

The youngest brother knocked on the door of the inn. He asked for a room for the night. He was given the key to the stable and a braid of hair. He led his horse, and carried the cat, into the stable. There he saw the lion and horse of the huntsman, and the horse and dog of the middle brother. He gave his horse hay and set his cat loose to find mice. He took out his hunting knife and cut the hair braid into small pieces. Then he cut loose the horses, the lion, and the dog, and he also cut their hair braids into small pieces. He put all the pieces into his pocket, and went back into the inn.

"Where are my brothers?"

"You'll have to fight me to know!"

They began to fight. The magician began to win.

"Come, horses! Come, Lion! Come, Dog! Come, Cat! Come and save your masters!"

"Braid of hair, grow thick!"

At that the youngest brother pulled all the pieces of hair out of his pocket and pushed them into the magician's mouth. As the braid grew thick the evil innkeeper swelled up like a toad and he burst into pieces.

The horses, the lion, the dog, and the cat came from the stable. The evil spells on the brothers melted, and the young men came down to meet their youngest brother.

The three rode out of the inn and back to the woman washing.

"Are you washing still?" they called.

"If I want to eat," she said.

The boys laughed at the poor washerwoman. She would have been angry, but they told her to give up washing and go to the tower, and there to take up the career of innkeeper.

And to this day she keeps that inn, high on the mountain road, and if you stop there and ask for a room, she'll tell you this story.

In Palos de Moguer

On the southwestern coast of Spain there is a salty river, the Río Saltés, that empties into the Atlantic. Up that salty river, past a marsh, lay the joining of two rivers. One was the Odiel (Oh-thee-EHL), the river on which the large city of Huelva is located. The other was the Tinto (TEEN-toh), and on it were the towns of Moguer and Palos. Palos was sometimes called Palos de Moguer because it was close to Moguer. It was sometimes called Palos de la Frontera, because it was at the very frontier, the edge of the known world.

Most of the sailors on Columbus's three ships had come from the towns along these rivers, which provided good harbors for ships to rest in, away from the stormy Atlantic.

Black-and-Yellow

The sun was beginning to rise over the town of Palos de Moguer where the wives and sisters and daughters and young sons of the Pinzón families were awaiting their menfolk's return. The families were up and the breakfasts were cooking on the fires. While she stirred the pot, one grandmother told the young children their favorite fairy tale.

It was that there was a little hill in the southern mountains of Spain that looked very much like the little loaf of fresh bread your grandmother just took out of the oven—a little *panecillo (pah-neh-SEEL-yoh)*, but, of course, it was as big as a hill. On either side of this little *"panecillo"* there was a little village.

To the east of the hill was a little village where everyone dressed all in yellow—from their caps to their shoes, all in yellow. Their banner was a little yellow flag, and their gardens were full of yellow flowers. The people of the town were always at play. They never did any work at all; every day was a holiday and every meal was a picnic. Everyone laughed and sang and danced and played their guitars. But something was missing from their lives.

On the west side of the little round mountain was another village, where everyone dressed all in black— from their hoods to their boots, all in black. Their flag was a little black banner, and their pots and their kettles and their hinges and door handles were all of the finest, shiniest black iron. The people of the town were always at work. They never played at all; every day was a workday. The men were always sawing or hammering; the women were always working in the homes, sweeping the floors. If the floors were clean they swept the paths to their front stoops, and if the paths were clean they went out and swept the cobblestone streets. Everyone was solemn and silent and serious, and very, very hard at work. But if you asked them if they were happy, they would say, "We cannot know, for we are always working. We have nothing to compare it to."

One day a great wise man was walking along the winding road through the mountains of southern Spain, when he came to the little village where everyone dressed all in yellow. He saw them laughing and singing and dancing, and playing their guitars. Because he was wise and valued wisdom above all else, he asked the people a question. It took a long time to quiet the people so they could hear him in the village square, or plaza. Finally he asked them if they were happy. They said, "We cannot know, for we are always playing. We have nothing to compare it to."

The wise man was troubled by their answer, but he went on and walked around the little round mountain until he came to the village where everyone was dressed all in black. He saw them gardening and cleaning and chopping wood and polishing the ironwork grills on the windows of their houses. Everyone was solemn, silent, and serious, but the wise man knew something was missing from these people's lives.

Then he knew he must do something very wise to help the people in these two villages find happiness. The wise man knew many things, and he also knew all the right magic words. (I am sorry to say that in the many centuries that have passed since this story happened, most of the magic in the world has melted in the morning sun and floated away on the mist, but this was long ago, and the wise man knew powerful magic words.) He made his plan.

The wise man stood in the plaza of the village where everyone was dressed all in black.

"*Señores (Sehn-YOHR-ehs)* and *señoras (sehn-YOHR-ahs)*, let me have your attention, please. Tomorrow morning I will be on the top of the *panecillo*, and if you will meet me there we will do some work together!"

All the people nodded and said, "It is good. We would like to do some new work for a change. Tomorrow, in the morning, we will be there."

Then the wise man went back around the little mountain to the plaza of the village where everyone was dressed all in yellow. He called to them, and they grew quiet and heard him say:

"*Señores* and *señoras*, let me have your attention, please. Tomorrow morning I will be on top of the *panecillo*, and if you will meet me there we will have a party together."

All the people laughed and sang and danced and played their guitars, and said, "It is good. We would like to have a party on a mountaintop. Tomorrow, in the morning, we will be there."

As the sun rose over the mountains of southern Spain and the first beam of sunlight struck the little round mountain, there sat the wise man with his legs crossed and his arms folded. Up the eastern side of the mountain came the people all dressed in yellow, laughing and singing and dancing, and carrying picnic baskets and guitars. Up the western side of the mountain came the people all dressed in black, carrying axes and hammers and gardening tools for whatever kind of civic work might be required on a mountaintop. When the people all dressed in yellow saw the people all dressed in black, they began to shout insults at each other and shake their fists in the air.

The people in black shook their fingers at the other villagers and shouted, "Lazy! Loafers! Worthless ones!"

The people in yellow thumbed their noses at the other villagers and shouted, "Homebodies! Party spoilers! Stuck-in-the-muds!"

Pretty soon all the people were quarreling and fighting and poking each other. The wise man unfolded his arms, raised his hands high, and said the most powerful magic word he knew. Suddenly, no one was dressed all in yellow, and no one was dressed all in black.

Now everyone was dressed the same: one stripe of yellow, one stripe of black, one stripe of yellow, one stripe of black. And now no one wanted to work all the time and no one wanted to play all the time. Now they all agreed.

When the sun was high and yellow in the sky, the people went out to work in their gardens or in the fields, but they laughed and talked as they worked, and they sang going to and from the fields. When the womenfolk brought lunch to the menfolk in the fields they made a picnic of it.

When night fell, and the sky was black and the streets were dark with shadows, the people went into their houses or into the plaza and danced and played their guitars around the yellow light of candles and lanterns.

Now the people were happy, for they had both work and play to give variety to their days, and could compare the two. As the years rolled by and turned into centuries, the magic in the world melted in the morning sun and floated away in the mist. As the magic evaporated, these people grew smaller and smaller, until they were no bigger than your thumbnail. They left their villages and moved into little round mounds like the little round mountain, only more the size of a little loaf of grandmother's fresh bread. When the sun is high and yellow in the sky these people come out with the morning sun and float into the air like the morning mist. They fly to the fields and gather harvest from the flowers. When the sky is black with night, they fly back to their little round house, bringing home the pollen and nectar they have harvested. They sing and dance around their little house, and they play on tiny guitars.

These little people are the bees. There were no bees in the world until the wise man said that magic word. And I know the story to be true, because my grandfather told it to me.

The Young Lovers from Teruel

One of the older girls, a daughter of one Columbus's captains, told another story as the breakfast finished cooking. She told of the Young Lovers from Teruel.

It happened that there were, in the village of Teruel *(Tehr-WELL)* in the Kingdom of Aragón *(Ah-rah-GOHN)*, two children—a boy and a girl—whose families' mansions were side by side. Both families were noble, but one family still had all their wealth, while the other family had fallen on hard times, as sometimes happened to noble families in the ancient days. The little girl's family was very rich, but the little boy's family was quite poor, in spite of the large house in which they lived. The children played together and became great friends, and both being of noble birth, their families approved of their friendship.

As the years passed the friendship turned to love, and the poor *hidalgo (ee-DAHL-goh)*, a young nobleman, named Diego asked the lovely *doncella (dohn-SELL-yah)*, a young lady, named Isabel for her hand in marriage. While Isabel freely consented, being very much in love with Diego, her father refused to give his permission because Diego's family was so poor.

Diego protested that keeping them apart would break their hearts, but the girl's father would not change his mind. All seemed lost for the young lovers from Teruel. At last, after Isabel begged her father to think it over, he agreed that if Diego would go out into the world and earn a fortune in six years time, he would give his permission for the two to marry.

Diego asked the nobleman to promise him he would not give his daughter's hand in marriage to anyone else for six years, to give Diego a chance to earn a fortune and win his beloved's hand. The girl's father agreed.

Young Diego could think of only one way to win a fortune in so short a time. There was a great war being fought in the Near East, where knights of the Christian faith fought warriors of the Moslem faith over the right to rule the city of Jerusalem, the city of the Bible, sacred to the Jewish people, the Moslems, and the Christians. Diego joined the army of knights going on a crusade. (This great War of the Cross lasted many years and was one of four such Wars of the Cross fought in the twelfth and thirteenth centuries.)

In the years that followed, Diego became a knight himself, and served valiantly in the war. He was made a captain of the army, then a commander. In every battle he thought only of his beloved Isabel, and the memory of her made him ride faster and fight harder than any of the other knights. In those days, when knights from all over Europe won a battle against a walled city, they would demand a heavy tax from the conquered city to pay their way onward to Jerusalem. Soon Diego had won many prizes, been given many gifts, and collected a great many taxes from cities he had conquered. Soon he had a great treasure, loaded in wooden chests which he carried in an oxcart.

It was time to return to Aragón, to the city of Teruel, and claim his beloved. The journey home was long, and the treasure carts moved slowly. Years had passed, and Diego's time was running out. Finally it was one day before the sixth anniversary of his departure to go on the crusade, and he was not yet home. He struggled over the dirt roads, as fast as he was able to go, as the sun rose on the last day of Isabel's father's promise.

Diego was still one day's journey from Teruel!

Back at his mansion, Isabel's father had counted the days very carefully and knew that the time for keeping his promise was nearly at an end. He went into the bedchamber of his daughter and told her what day it was. He also reminded her that in all the six years she had never received any news of Diego (who had been too far away and in circumstances too dangerous to write a letter or send a message.) He reminded her that, for all they knew, Diego might have died years ago in the war in that faraway land.

Isabel wept quietly. She feared that her father spoke the truth—that, in fact, her Diego was probably among the dead of that long and bitter war.

Her father told Isabel that another nobleman, Azagra *(Ah-SAH-grah)* by name, had recently asked for her hand in marriage, and that he had given his permission, provided the six-year promise had come to an end. Isabel sadly agreed that when the six years were up, she would marry Azagra, who was wealthy and handsome.

When the anniversary day came and the six years had ended, the wedding feast was held in the mansion of Don Azagra. Not far away, along the dusty road, Diego was coming closer—one day too late. The wedding took place and the families embraced each other and rejoiced. The wedding guests ate and drank and sang and danced. But Isabel was sad, and asked her husband to understand why she wanted to sleep alone that night in a quiet room. Don Azagra was a kind man and loved Doña Isabel very much, so he agreed to stay and entertain the guests while she went upstairs to sleep in a quiet bedchamber.

In the privacy of her room, Isabel sat by the fire and sang softly to herself, happy to be married to so kind a man, but sad at the loss of her beloved Diego. Just at that moment, like the dreams she had been having for six years, Diego stepped into her bedchamber. He had arrived at Teruel, one day late, and gone straight to the mansion of Isabel's family where the servants, who did not recognize him, told him of the wedding at the mansion of Don Azagra. Climbing the vines on the columns of the porch, Diego entered the room—the last steps of a journey of thousands of leagues.

Doña Isabel gasped at the sight of him—older, bearded, greying, and dirty from the road. She did not recognize him! He spoke and she almost fainted.

Diego fell to his knees and told her of the long journey, of the years on the path of war, of his inability to send word home, of the hundred battles and the thousand times he had risked his life to earn a fortune for the two of them to live on throughout their life together. He told of coming home, of visiting her mansion without even going to his own home, of learning of the wedding from the servants, and of passing unrecognized through the wedding guests to climb to her chamber.

He begged her for one kiss, one last kiss.

She wept and held his hand in hers. She was married now, to an honorable man, and she would not break the promises she had made in the wedding ceremony only hours before.

Isabel loved Diego more than she loved her own life, but she had made vows before God in the wedding ceremony, and her duty now was to her kind Azagra. If Diego had come only one day earlier, she would have greeted him not with one kiss, but with one thousand kisses. Now they both knew it was too late.

Diego, on his knees before her and still holding her hand, bowed his head in sorrow. He clutched at his heart with his other hand and fell at her feet, dead of a broken heart. Diego, the son of the nobleman García *(Gahr-SEE-ah)*, was no more.

Isabel wept bitterly and released his hand from hers, laying it across his chest on the dusty tabard with its bright red cross. She knelt beside him, folded her hands, and began to pray for his soul.

Much later, Don Azagra came to her door to see if she were well; one of the servants had heard her crying. She greeted him and told him that she had had a nightmare. She said she had dreamed that Don Diego came back from the crusades and wanted one last kiss. She said she had dreamed that she refused him, and his heart broke and he fell dead at her feet. She asked what her new husband thought she should have done had this happened for real, instead of in a dream.

Knowing of his new bride's love for Don Diego, and being a kind man, Don Azagra smiled. He said if it had happened in real life he would have understood, and she would have been permitted to give her former lover one last kiss. At this, Doña Isabel burst into tears. She told Don Azagra it had not been a dream. Don Diego lay dead in her bedchamber.

Sadly, Don Azagra and a trusted servant lifted the body of Don Diego and carried it to the front door of Don García's mansion. They laid the body down carefully, so it looked as if Don Diego, tired and worn out from the war and the long journey home, had died of relief just as he was about to enter his own home. The treasure carts he had brought with him would make his poor family wealthy once more. He had been a good son and a dear friend.

The funeral was held the following day, and all the people of Teruel went to the burial in the churchyard. Don Azagra and Doña Isabel went also, dressed in the black clothing of mourning. Just before the casket was to be closed and lowered into the ground, Doña Isabel stepped forward and bent over the body of her former childhood sweetheart. She spoke softly to the body, saying that she had brought him the one last kiss he had requested the night before. She kissed Don Diego goodbye and laid her head on the chest of the man who was to have been her husband.

When Doña Isabel did not stand after a long while, Don Azagra rushed forward to her.

Doña Isabel had died, her own heart broken, resting her head on the chest of Don Diego. They were buried side by side in stone tombs, in their village in Aragón, a town that has never forgotten the young lovers from Teruel.

In Genoa

East of the port from which Columbus sailed, Palos de Moguer, east of the Río Saltés down which his ships had sailed to reach the Atlantic, eastward along the coastline of the Mediterranean Sea, lies Genoa. Columbus was born in Genoa, in what we now call Italy. Along the wharfs and piers of the city there were inns that sold food and wine.

Sailors, perhaps men who knew Columbus in his youth, were sitting at breakfast on a wooden table beside a warm fire. They were laughing and telling rude stories as they ate their wheat cakes and olive oil.

Madonna Francesca

Many stories tell of young women who do not sit idly by waiting for "prince charming" to come along. This is a silly story about a young woman who took matters into her own hands!

Madonna Francesca *(Mah-DOH-nah Frahn-CHESS-kah)* was a beautiful lady, and every man wanted to become her husband. Handsome men came to court her, but there also came men who were too old, or too ugly, or too smelly, or too stupid, and she wanted to get rid of these men as quickly as possible. What she wanted most of all was a man who was smart! But she hadn't met the right man yet.

One day there came to call at her villa a man named Rinuccio *(Ree-NOO-choh)* who was so unpleasant that he had been kicked out of his hometown of Florence. He was rude and had bad manners, and picked his nose. Francesca did not like him a bit, and she did not let him visit her long.

Another day there came a caller named Alessandro *(Ah-lehss-SAHN-droh),* who had also been run out of the town of Florence, and this fellow was even worse than the first. The two men didn't know each other, and didn't know that they had both seen Francesca from a distance and decided to try to win her hand in marriage. Francesca cut Alessandro's visit short, too.

That evening, she was talking with her maidservant about the events of the day.

"Two unpleasant men came to call on me today," said Madonna Francesca. "I don't like either of them, and I wish they would not come to visit me again."

"Speaking of unpleasant," said the maidservant, "did you hear that old man Scannadio *(Skah-NAH-joh)* died today? He was the ugliest man in Pistoia *(Pee-STOH-yah),* and he looked so awful that some people fainted when they saw him in his casket."

Don Scannadio had been buried in a stone tomb above ground in the courtyard of the church of the minor friars, an order of monks who cared for the poor, the friendless, and, in this case, the very ugly. Madonna Francesca got an idea as she listened to her maidservant tell of how ugly the late Don Scannadio had looked in his casket.

"I have an idea," said the lovely lady. "The next time those two unpleasant Florentines come for a visit, I will put them to a test, and if they fail the test they must go away and leave me alone."

The lady and her maidservant talked for hours, making their plan.

The next day, when Alessandro came to call on Madonna Francesca the maid greeted him at the door and said, "My Lady is in much distress and cannot see you today. Her dear Uncle Scannadio..." (Here the maid tried not to laugh, for Francesca was in no way related to the old man.) "…was buried yesterday in the courtyard of the church of the minor friars, in the great tomb. No one has paid the fee yet for burying him there, and his body may have to be removed and brought here. If you love My Lady, she will consent to be your bride if you can pass this test of bravery: go in darkness tonight and unwrap Don Scannadio from his grave shroud. Then wrap yourself in the shroud and lie down in his place. When the relatives come to carry the body away, it will be you they bring here, and poor Uncle Scannadio may continue to rest in peace in the tomb."

Although Alessandro was disgusted by the thought of unwrapping a corpse and lying beside it, he agreed to do so in order to win the hand of Madonna Francesca.

"But," warned the maidservant, "if you fail in this dangerous deed, My Lady will be very disappointed and will never want to see you again."

Alessandro left.

A little later Rinuccio came by with a bouquet of ugly, wilted flowers for Francesca. The maid met him at the door.

"My Lady is in much distress and cannot see you today. Her beloved Uncle Scannadio…" (Again, the maid tried not to laugh at the thought of lovely Francesca being related to ugly old Don Scannadio.) "…died today. His body was placed in the tomb in the courtyard of the church of the minor friars, but My Lady cannot afford to purchase a place in that tomb, and the body will have to be returned here. You must go to the tomb at midnight and lift the body out of its coffin, and bring it here.

"My Lady is embarrassed at not having enough money to pay for the tomb space and she doesn't want anyone to see you bring the body back here. If you succeed in this dangerous task, My Lady will be very pleased with you. But if you fail, she will be very disappointed in you and will never want to see you again."

Rinuccio was disgusted at the thought of carrying a dead body all the way back from the cemetery, but he agreed to try, and he left.

The maid and Madonna Francesca laughed over the trick they had arranged.

As night fell, Alessandro went toward the courtyard of the church of the minor friars. He sneaked into the graveyard and went to the huge stone tomb. He opened the heavy wooden door and went in to the dark interior of the tomb. All around were coffins of stone, resting on the floor and stacked along the wall. How would he know which was the coffin of old Scannadio?

The only coffin that had not yet gathered any dust was that of old Scannadio. Alessandro lifted the heavy lid and trembled as he looked in at the dead old man wrapped in a white grave shroud. He set the lid beside the coffin and lifted the corpse out. He unwrapped the dead man from the grave shroud of white linen.

Scannadio was even uglier dead than he had been alive!

Alessandro wrapped himself in the shroud and laid down beside the dead man, covering the corpse with some loose ends of the shroud so that only Alessandro would be noticed in the coffin. Then he pulled the lid over the coffin and lay there in the dark.

For a moment he imagined what it would be like if the dead man should become angry or cold, and strangle him to get the shroud back. When those fears passed, he thought about someone finding out that he had opened a coffin, and arresting him and burning him at the stake for his crime. But that fear passed, too, and soon Alessandro fell asleep beside the dead old man.

As the midnight hour approached, a night watchman called out the hour, and Rinuccio slipped out of his house dressed in a dark cloak so he would be harder to see in the darkness. He sneaked to the courtyard of the minor friars and into the graveyard. Just as midnight came, he was opening the heavy wooden door of the tomb.

Rinuccio began to imagine what might happen if the night watchman should catch him entering a tomb at midnight. People would think he had come to rob the dead, and he would be sent to a dungeon! When those fears passed, he went inside. For a moment he thought he heard someone snore, but it must have been merely the creaking of the old wooden door as it opened.

Rinuccio found the coffin of Don Scannadio and opened it. Inside was a still body, wrapped in cloth. Slowly Rinuccio lifted the body onto his shoulders. It seemed awfully heavy for a dead old man.

Alessandro awoke! The family had come for him. He was being carried to the house of Madonna Francesca! He had to pretend to be dead.

Rinuccio couldn't see in the darkness and bumped Alessandro into a post, and a tree, and a gate, but Alessandro didn't make a sound. Rinuccio grumbled and complained about the weight of the body, but he didn't put Alessandro down, no matter how sore his back got.

The pair of fools were almost to Madonna Francesca's house when the night watchman of that street saw them.

Francesca and the maid could also see them, from the upstairs window of her villa.

"Halt!" called the watchman. "Who goes there?"

Rinuccio screamed and threw down the body in the shroud. He ran as fast as he could, all the way to his house, and never came back to that street again.

Alessandro hit the ground hard when Rinuccio dropped him, and let out a scream. He ran in the opposite direction as fast as he could, tripping all the way on the folds of the grave shroud. He never came back to that street again.

The night watchman saw the body in the shroud get up, and thinking it was a ghost, he let out a scream and ran in another direction. He gave up his job as night watchman, and never came out at night again.

Madonna Francesca and her maid laughed until tears ran down their faces and went to bed happy to be rid of the two foolish men.

Bastianello

Rough men enjoy telling stories about how foolish some other man is. The story of Bastianello (Bahs-tee-ah-NEH-loh) is a good example of the story sometimes called "The Three Sillies."

Some people are such fools! And this is the story of a family that was full of them. In the town just over the mountain from ours, there lived a foolish man named Sebastiano *(Seh-bahst-YAH-noh)* with his foolish wife Stulta *(STOOL-tah)*. They had a daughter named Carmella, who was lovely but a little silly.

A local farmboy asked Carmella for her hand in marriage and she accepted. So the boy went to Sebastiano and asked for his permission to marry the girl. When Sebastiano and Stulta had given permission, a great wedding feast was planned. One thing they wanted to have was enough good wine to drink at the feast, for the water in the village well was full of toads and no good to drink. Sebastiano bought three barrels of good red wine, and had them rolled into the cellar under the house.

The whole village, including many people who weren't even invited, gathered for the wedding feast, and everyone sat down to eat and drink before the wedding ceremony. Soon everyone had drunk their wine and there was no more in the pitchers to serve the guests. Carmella wanted to show what a good wife she was going to be to Giuseppe *(Joo-SEHP-pih),* the farmboy, so she volunteered to go to the basement and get more wine. She took the pitchers and walked down the spiral stone staircase to the basement.

She put the first pitcher under the spigot set into the barrel and turned it open. The wine began to flow out of the barrel into the pitcher. As she waited for the pitcher to fill, Carmella began to daydream.

"When this pitcher is full, I will go upstairs," she thought, "and when the meal is over, I will be married. When the ceremony is over, Giuseppe and I will move to a farmhouse and set up housekeeping, and soon I'll have a fine baby son and we will name him Bastianello, 'Little Sebastiano,' after my dear father. When he grows up he will be a soldier and go off to war. But if he should die, oh, how I would cry!"

At the thought of little Bastianello, who wasn't even born yet, dying in a battle, Carmella began to cry and cry. The wine pitcher was full, and the wine kept flowing out of the barrel. The wine overflowed the pitcher and ran onto the basement floor. Carmella cried and cried for poor Bastianello, who had died in a battle and hadn't been born yet!

After a while, the guests were getting thirsty and Stulta said, "I'll go down and see what's keeping our daughter." She went down the spiral stone staircase into the cellar. There was Carmella, crying and crying, with the wine up to her ankles on the cellar floor.

"Why are you crying?" asked Stulta.

"I daydreamed I was married and had a son named Bastianello. He became a soldier and he died in a battle!" said Carmella.

"Oh, my poor grandson, killed in a battle," moaned Stulta, "and him not even born yet!" She began to cry and cry, and the wine kept pouring out of the barrel onto the floor of the cellar.

After a while, the guests at the feast were getting really thirsty, so Sebastiano said, "I'll go down and see what's keeping my wife and daughter."

Down the spiral stone staircase he went into the cellar. There stood Stulta and Carmella, crying and crying, with the wine up to their calves on the cellar floor.

"Why are you crying?" asked Sebastiano.

Stulta said, "Carmella daydreamed she was married and had a son named Bastianello. He became a soldier and was killed in a battle!"

"Oh, my poor namesake, killed in a battle," gasped Sebastiano, "and him not even born yet!" He, too, began to cry and cry, and the wine kept pouring out of the barrel onto the floor of the cellar.

After a while, the guests at the feast upstairs were as dry as wheat chaff, and the groom said, "I'll go down and see what's keeping my bride-to-be, and my mother-in-law-to-be, and my father-in-law-to-be."

Down he went, down the spiral stone staircase into the cellar, where he stepped into a pool of red wine. There stood Carmella, Stulta, and Sebastiano, crying and crying.

"Why are you crying?" asked Giuseppe.

Sebastiano said, "Carmella dreamed you and she were married, and you had a son named Bastianello. He became a soldier and died in a battle!"

Giuseppe waded through the wine, which came up to his knees on the cellar floor, and turned off the spigot in the barrel.

"You three are such sillies!" he shouted. "I cannot marry your daughter," he said to Sebastiano and Stulta. "I will go out into the world and seek my fortune. I would not come back here unless I found three people sillier than you."

With that, Giuseppe turned around in the wine and waded back to the stairs. His shoes squished as he climbed back up to the feast.

"Where's the wine?" called the guests.

"It's in the cellar," said Giuseppe. "Go drown in it!"

As he left the house, he could hear the guests laughing and splashing in the cellar, swimming in the wine, and trying to console the foolish family who were crying over their poor dead grandson who hadn't been born yet.

Giuseppe went to his house and packed all his belongings in a spare linen handkerchief. Everything fit nicely, because all he owned was a spare linen handkerchief. He also put in a loaf of bread and a flask of wine that his mother and father gave him. The next morning he set out to seek his fortune, with his belongings tied in a bundle on a stick.

Off he went down the road. He came to the village well, which was full of toads. Beside the well was a man with a water jar full of toads and a copper sieve all full of holes. He was lowering the sieve into the well, bringing it up, and pouring the water into the jar. But all the water ran out by the time he got the sieve to the top of the well, and just about all that went into the jar was an occasional toad.

"What are you doing, Uncle?" asked Giuseppe, even though he was not related to the man.

"Filling my jar with this sieve," he answered. "But it is taking me a great long while."

"No, Uncle," said Giuseppe, "you don't get water in a sieve. You get water in a bucket."

With that, Giuseppe went to a neighboring house and borrowed a bucket. Soon the jar was full and all the toads swam out over the rim and hopped away.

The man thanked Giuseppe, and Giuseppe walked away thinking, "Well, there's one man sillier than my in-laws-to-have-been!"

Giuseppe went a little further. This was a whole village of people who were not too bright, and he soon came upon a man sitting in a tree with his stockings on, jumping to the ground near a pair of leather boots.

"What are you doing, Uncle?" asked Giuseppe.

"Can't you see that I'm trying to put on my new boots?" asked the man as he climbed back up the tree, took aim, and jumped again, missing the boots entirely. "I've been at this a great long while, but I still can't get them on."

"No, Uncle," said Giuseppe, "you don't put on boots that way. You do it like this."

With that, Giuseppe took off his own boots and set them aside, and pulled on the man's leather boots one at a time. When he had the man's boots on he said, "See?"

"Say," said the foolish man, "that looks easy!" He took Giuseppe's boots and put them on one at a time, just as Giuseppe had done.

"Say," said the foolish man, "these boots don't fit me at all."

After Giuseppe got the man's boots off, and took his own boots off the man's feet, and put his own boots back on, which took quite a while in itself, the man thanked Giuseppe. Giuseppe went away thinking, "Well, that's another man sillier than my in-laws-to-have-been!"

Giuseppe went on a little further, but remember, this was an entire community of knotheads. He soon came to a wedding party just outside the gate to the churchyard. There he saw a groom on foot and his bride-to-be riding a fine white horse. The bride was so tall in the saddle of the great war horse that she could not ride under the crosspiece above the gateposts. Everyone was standing around, scratching their heads.

"What are you doing, Cousins?" asked Giuseppe.

"We are supposed to be married," said the groom, "but we can't get into the church. My bride-to-be can't ride under the crosspiece over the gateposts. She's too tall."

"Cut the horse's legs off shorter," suggested one wedding guest.

"No, no," said another guest, "cut the bride's head off."

"This isn't much of a wedding, anyway," said another guest. "I heard there was a wedding yesterday where they filled the whole cellar with wine! I'd go there instead, only it was yesterday."

"No, Cousins," said Giuseppe, "you don't cut off the horse's legs or the bride's head."

Giuseppe walked up to the horse, and turned and said to the groom-to-be, "Let me kiss the bride."

When the girl bent over to kiss Giuseppe, he slapped the horse's rump and the horse ran through the gate before the bride could sit back up. Everyone ran through the gate and into the church, cheering. The groom thanked Giuseppe and shook his hand for quite a while. Giuseppe went away thinking, "Maybe I didn't have it so bad after all."

With that, he took all his worldly possessions and his loaf of bread and his flask of wine, and went back to the house of his bride-to-be. There he found Sebastiano chiselling a marble gravestone that said 'Bastianello' on it, just in case Giuseppe came back, and married Carmella, and they had a son named Bastianello, and he became a soldier and was killed in a battle.

"Well, I'm back," said Giuseppe to Carmella, who came out to greet him all dressed in black to mourn her poor son who had died in battle before he had even had a chance to be born.

They were married and had a fine son named Bastianello. He became a city councilman, so he was never troubled with having to work or think a difficult thought in his life. And as for that marble tombstone—well, he just used it as a paperweight until his desk fell through into the cellar of the city hall where all the wine barrels were stored.

And I moved out of that village, with all my belongings bundled up in my spare linen handkerchief, and came here to tell you the story of Bastianello.

The Stories behind the Stories

- **Don Juan Calderón Kills Seven** (Very Important Mr. Johnny Cooking-Pot Kills Seven.) This fairy tale was told all over Europe with many different names and events. It is sometimes called "The Little Tailor."

- **The Cave of the Inaja-Palm Paint** is a retelling of the creation myth of the Taino people. Christopher Columbus himself asked a Catalán Spanish priest named Ramón Pané to record some of the beliefs of the Taino people in 1495. A copy of his manuscript of their legends is in the Library of the Museum of Anthropology in Mexico City, where these editors read it and prepared this edited translation.

- The Columbus ship and historical material is gleaned from many sources: *The Columbus Diary,* as transcribed (before the original disappeared from a monastery library) by Bartolomé de Las Casas; Columbus's letter to Rafael Sánchez, written on board the *Niña* (after the *Santa María* sank) on the way back to Spain, from the facsimile printed by The W.H. Lowdermilk Co., Chicago, 1893; the letter from Diego Colón (Columbus's son) to Bartolomé de las Casas, in 1519; and the letter from Diego to Ximénez de Cisneros, Cardinal Archbishop of Toledo, Spain, sent from Hispaniola on January 12, 1512. Both of the Colón letters are in the Gilcrease Museum in Tulsa, Oklahoma, where the editors of this collection read them.

- **The Cat Who Became A Monk**,
- **The Pig and the Mule**,
- **The House Mouse and the Field Mouse**, and
- **Lady Owl's Child** all come from *The Book of Cats,* a well-known Spanish translation, done in about 1420, of the fables of Odo of Cheriton, an English monk.

- ***The Example of the Lion and the Rabbit*** is from the *Book of Kalila and Dimna,* a very long *enxiemplo* (ancient fable or "example") collection that allegorically describes life at the Mongol Court in the twelfth century. The work was translated from the original Sanscrit into Pelehvi for reading in Persia, and from Pelehvi into Arabic for reading in Arabia. In 1251, King Alfonso the Wise of Castille ordered the Arabic version translated into Spanish, making it the first book of stories and fables ever written in Old Spanish.

- ***The Smoking Mountain*** is one version of a story that has been told orally in Mexico among the Náhuatl-speaking people for seven centuries. In one version the lovers are both royal; other variants have other details. It is impossible to know which variant was actually told in 1492. The editors have chosen a version which they learned in Mexico in 1971.

- ***Hungry Coyote's Lament*** was composed in the Náhuatl language of the Aztec people. It was translated into Spanish in the 1500s. The modern Spanish version quoted by Prescott in *The Conquest of Mexico* was consulted for this newly edited translation for young readers.

- ***Wailing Woman*** is a purely Mexican story that has spread throughout Central America and the American Southwest. Modern descendants of the Aztecs claim it was originally an Aztec story, but scholars disagree on its original content, and on which Aztec figures or goddesses may be represented in the folktale version. The editors have chosen a version told by Náhuatl speakers in Mexico today, who reconstruct what they believe to have been their ancestors' version of the story.

- ***Skeleton's Revenge*** is a story told in Mexico City about a gambling nobleman who kills a priest. The events are supposed to have happened in the 1600s or early 1700s in Tlatelolco, but some Indian people tell it as though it happened to *patolli* players in pre-conquest times. The editors have chosen to reconstruct this version and present it as a possible precursor to the Spanish colonial legend.

- ***The Chests of Sand*** is an excerpt from the long *cantar de gesta* about the Spanish "crusader" knight Rodrigo Díaz de Bivar. It was composed after the events took place in the 1090s, and memorized and recited by troubadors for centuries afterwards.

- *El Cid and the Lion* takes place at the beginning of Book Eight of *El cantar de mío Cid.*

- *The Tree of Life* is a Carib creation myth, part of a longer cycle of events involving twin sons of the sun, Pia and Makunaima.

- *The Iron Dancing Shoes* is a Portuguese retelling of a common European legend that my have originally come from India by way of the Moors. The Moors invaded the Iberian Peninsula in 711, bringing to Spain and Portugal the culture of the Near East and India.

- *The Three Citrons of Love* is a Portuguese retelling of another common European legend that may have come from India or the Near East originally.

- *The Tower of Ill Fortune* is a Portuguese retelling of another common European legend that may have originally come from the Near East or India.

- *Black-And-Yellow* is one version of "The Bees," an ancient Spanish how-and-why story, usually known as *"Las Abejas."* This and some of the other Spanish stories were first heard by the editor in Quito, Ecuador, (the most provincial of South American countries) in 1953 and 1954.

- *The Young Lovers of Teruel* is the best-known Spanish love story, possibly based on true events that happened in or about the year 1200.

- *Madonna Francesca* is the First Tale of the Ninth Day in *The Decameron,* a collection of one hundred folktales on bawdy themes, composed by Giovanni Boccaccio from stories that were already old when he wrote them down in the 1300s.

- *Bastianello* is a very old folktale, also called "The Perfect Fool," which was well-known and told for centuries before it was written down in *The Pentameron* by Basile in 1634.

Glossary

This glossary will help you understand the words and foreign names used in these stories. Very common words and names, like Christopher Columbus, can be found in dictionaries and encyclopedias in your classroom, home, or library.

- *Agouti* A brown-haired rodent much like a squirrel.

- *Alcázar* The name given to many castles built by the Moorish kings of small kingdoms in what is now modern Spain.

- *Annatto* A kind of plant the Mexicans call *achiote (ah-chee-OH-teh).* A red dye made from the annatto tree, a tropical tree that has red seeds.

- *Aragón* One of the small kingdoms in what would later become Spain.

- *Arlanzón* A river with a bridge over it, located outside the city of Burgos.

- *Astride* In the position to ride. When someone leaps astride a horse, he jumps onto the horse and lands ready to ride at once.

- *Aztec* The Aztec civilization was a warlike tribe of Mexican Indians who overthrew their masters, the Toltecs, and became the most important tribe and civilization in Central Mexico from 1300 to 1521 A.D.

- **Bivar** Also spelled Vivar. El Cid's castle in northern Spain in 1094.

- **Búcar** A Moorish king from a small kingdom in North Africa. He was an enemy of El Cid.

- **Burgos** The old capital city of Spain in 1094.

- **Caballero** A gentleman. "Horseman" in Spanish.

- **Caliph** The king and religious leader of a Moslem country.

- **Canary Islands** A chain of small islands off the coast of northwest Africa that belonged to Spain in 1492. These islands are also called the Canaries, and it is from these islands that the birds called canaries get their name.

- **Carib** A tribe of Indians who lived on the northern coast of South America in what is now called Venezuela. Enemies of the Taino.

- **Carrión** A small principality (a castle with a prince and lands) in the old kingdom of León. The sons of the prince were called by the title *infantes* (royal children) instead of "princes."

- **Cassava** The same plant as manioc comes from.

- **Castille** A region of modern Spain that was once a separate kingdom.

- **Causeway** A road built up out of the water. Stone and dirt were piled into the lake to make a firm, dry roadbed, like a levee or dam.

- **Cinched** Pulled tight. Old-fashioned belts did not buckle the way your belt does. Some belts were tied, and some were pulled tight in such a way that the leather held onto itself.

- **Conquerors** The winners in a war.

- **Crusade** A war in which Christian knights, wearing crosses as their "personal flags," fought against non-Christians, usually Moslems. The Moslems took the Holy Land away from the Christians and Jews around 1000 A.D., and Christians fought four great wars (crusades) against them in the 1100s and 1200s. The Christians also fought the Moslems in Spain from 718 until 1492. While the European Christians lost the four crusades to the Holy Land, the Christians won the crusade for the reconquest (winning back) of Spain.

- *Decree* An order given by a king, which everyone had to obey.

- *Defiantly* With anger, daring someone to try to stop you.

- *Doncella* A young noble lady.

- *Exile* Being told to leave and not return. This was a common punishment when someone had committed a crime.

- *Flint Road* The sad road traveled by Aztecs after death. The sharp flint rocks cut the flesh from the dead soul, and he arrived in the Land of the Dead as nothing but an unhappy skeleton.

- *Florence* A town in Italy. It is large and very famous.

- *Forecastle* The lookout post on a short tower at the front of a ship.

- *Galicia* A province in northern Spain, on the cold, stormy coast of the Cantabrian Sea.

- *Genoa* Columbus's home town on the northwest coast of Italy.

- *Granada* A large city in south-central Spain.

- *Guanahaní* The name the local Taino Indians gave to the island on which Columbus first landed.

- *Heaven of the Rain God* The Aztec rain god was Tláloc *(TLAH-lohk)*. The Aztecs believed that anyone who died in water went to a happy place like our heaven. The other dead, even good people, went to an unhappy place.

- *Hidalgo* A noble Spaniard, either rich or poor.

- *Inaja-Palm* A kind of palm tree that grows on the islands of the Caribbean Sea. A black body-paint can be made from this plant.

- **Inhabitants** The people who live there. If you lived in New York, you would be an inhabitant of New York.

- **Ixtaccíhuatl** "The Woman Lying Down" in the Aztec language. The name given to one of two volcanos on the eastern rim of the Valley of Mexico outside Mexico City.

- **La Gallega** "The Girl from Galicia," the nickname of Columbus's main ship, the *Santa María*.

- **Lagoon** A small lake that is right at a beach, and fills up with seawater. A freshwater lake very near the sea.

- **Lament** A sad song.

- **Leagues** Old-fashioned miles. A league was different in different countries and different centuries. A league could be as little as two-and-a-half miles, or as much as four-and-a-half miles.

- **Lord of the Dead** (Skeleton Man) The Aztec god of the unhappy land of the dead. When an Aztec died, it was believed he would travel a dangerous journey and end up in an unhappy place, no matter what kind of life he had lived.

- **Lucayas** The chain of islands in the Caribbean now known as the Greater Antilles.

- **Makunaima** One of two twin creator-gods of the Carib tribe.

- **Mango** A tropical fruit that looks and tastes a little like a sweet peach.

- **Manioc** A root from a plant. The root can be beaten into pulp and made into bread and other foods.

- **Maya** The Maya civilization was a tribe of Mexican Indians who lived in southeastern Mexico, in the area known as the Yucatán Peninsula.

- **Minor Friars** A group of monks who lived in a monastery.

- **Monasteries** Walled castles or churches where men go to be alone and serve God. The men are called monks, and often study to become priests.

- **Moors** Dark-skinned Moslem people from North Africa. Many Moors were friends with the people of Spain; others were their enemies.

- **Motecuhzoma** The Aztec name of two different kings of the Aztecs. We call them "Montezuma" because it's easier to say.

- **Nezahualcóyotl** "Hungry Coyote" in the Aztec language.

- **Nezahualpilli** "Hungry Prince" in the Aztec language.

- **Ornaments** Anything used as decoration is an ornament. We use ornaments on a tree at Christmas, but gold pins, earrings, noseplugs, and other decorations for clothes or for the body can also be called ornaments.

- **Oyoyotzín** One of the Aztec warrior-poets of the kingdom of Texcoco in the 1400s. He was a good friend of Nezahualcóyotl.

- **Palos De Moguer** A seaport town near the town of Moguer, in southern Spain in the province of Huelva. Columbus sailed from these towns on his first voyage to the New World in 1492.

- **Panecillo** "A little loaf of bread" in Spanish.

- **Papaya** A tropical fruit with orange insides that looks like a big green pear with black seeds. It tastes like a sour peach.

- **Patolli** A board game played by the Aztecs.

- **Peninsula** Spain and Portugal are two modern nations of Europe, located on a large piece of southwestern Europe that reaches out into the Atlantic Ocean. The people who live there call this land the Peninsula. Florida is another example of a peninsula.

- **Pennants** Long, narrow flags that flutter in the breeze. Lancers had pennants on their long, sharp lances. When they rode with the pennants up, it was like a modern army carrying its flag.

- **Pictograms** A way of writing by drawing pictures instead of writing letters of an alphabet. While pictograms do not communicate as precisely as written words do, they are very useful in societies that have not yet developed modern writing methods.

- **Pinzón** The last name of the family of Spanish shipbuilders and ship-owners who provided Columbus with ships.

- **Pistoia** A small town in Italy.

- **Popocatépetl** "The Smoking Mountain" in the Aztec language. The name given to the taller, active volcano on the eastern rim of the Valley of Mexico outside Mexico City. Ixtaccíhuatl is the other.

- **Procession** A parade of soldiers or important people.

- **Río Saltés** The Salty River, on the southwest coast of Spain, where the towns of Palos and Moguer are located.

- **Realm** Kingdom. A knight of the realm is a knight who serves the king of that kingdom.

- **Reap** Win or earn. Farmers also use this word to mean gather the crops.

- **Sacrificial Stone** The Aztecs believed that the sun was a hungry god who had to be fed. Men, women, and children were killed on stone altars as sacrifices or "gifts" to the sun-god. When the Christian Spaniards saw these awful human sacrifices, they wanted to destroy all the Aztec religion and civilization. The stones were huge round tables painted with human blood.

- **Santa Clara** "Saint Clara," the true name of Columbus's ship, the *Niña*.

- **Señor** "Sir" in Spanish.

- **Señores y Señoras** "Ladies and Gentlemen" in Spanish.

- **Shroud** The cloth, like a white bedsheet, that the dead were wrapped in. Today, we bury our dead in regular clothing.

- **Sieve** A bowl with holes in the bottom, used to drain wet vegetables or wet, cooked spaghetti.

- **Spigot** The old-fashioned faucet, made of wood, that was used to get wine out of a barrel.

- **Stucco** A hard covering for building walls that is put on like clay or mud and later dried by the sun.

- **Tabard** A cloth cover that a knight wore over his metal armor. There was a design on it that showed his rank and what army was his.

- **Tables** A board game played by knights in Europe in the Middle Ages (A.D. 1000 to 1500). The game was a lot like modern backgammon.

- **Taino** A now extinct tribe which once lived on the islands in the Caribbean Sea. The Tainos died of diseases that the Spaniards accidentally brought from Europe.

- **Tajo** The river that flows past the old Spanish capital city of Toledo

- **Tenochtitlán** "The Place of the Tenochca People," or "The Place of the Cactus-on-the-Stone" in the Aztec language. The name the Aztec Indians gave to their capital city on an island in a lake. Mexico City is built on the ruins of this earlier Aztec city.

- **Tépetl** "Mountain" in the Aztec language.

- **Teruel** An ancient city in Spain, 110 miles east of Madrid.

- **Texcoco** One of three Aztec cities in the Valley of Mexico that formed a triple kingdom with Tlacopán and Tenochtitlán.

- **Tlacopán** One of three Aztec cities in the Valley of Mexico that formed a triple kingdom with Tenochtitlán and Texcoco.

- **Tlatelolco** A small Indian city outisde Tenochtitlán. Today it is one neighborhood in Mexico City. Some of the magnificent Aztec pyramids and temples are visible as ruins there today.

- **Toledo** The former capital city of Spain.

- **Totoquil** One of three Aztec kings who ruled the triple kingdom while Nezahualcóyotl was alive. Totoquil was king of Tlacopán.

- **Turban** A small hat worn by some Moslem men. It is wrapped up in a long cloth that becomes the brim.

- *Tyranny* Cruel leadership.

- *Uncharted* Not yet mapped. No one had been to the New World yet, so there were no maps or charts of how to get there. This made the trip very dangerous.

- *Valiantly* Bravely and with honor.

- *Veteran* A former soldier. A retired warrior.

- *War horse* A very special kind of horse, almost twice as large and strong as a normal horse, that knights used in war. No normal horse could carry a knight and all his heavy armor.

- *Withered* All dried up and ugly, like a prune.

- *Yam* A plant root that looks and tastes a little like a long, orange sweet potato.

- *Yoloxóchitl* "Red Flower" in the Aztec language.

- *Yuca* Another type of plant like the cassava and manioc plant.